LET THERE BE LIGHT

Dan Gordon

BASED ON THE SCREENPLAY
BY SAM SORBO & DAN GORDON

REVEILLE PRESS
PO BOX 522251
Salt Lake City, UT 84152

www.lettherebelightmovie.com

Designed by Izzard Ink Publishing and Alissa Rose Theodor
Cover Design by Small Dog Design

Interior Photo Credit: All *Let There Be Light* film photos by Ginger McNamara, courtesy of LTBL Productions, LLC.

First Edition October 2017
Printed in the United States of America

Contact the author at info@izzardink.com.

Softback ISBN: 978-0-9828001-2-6
Hardback ISBN: 978-0-9828001-4-0
eBook ISBN: 978-0-9828001-3-3

To Sean Hannity for saying yes.

To Sam Sorbo for not taking no for an answer.

To Kevin Sorbo for having the good sense to marry Sam.

To Michael Franzese for entrusting me with truth he found in a 10x10 box, in the dark.

To Yoni Gordon who wrote a magnificent song.

To Damon Elliott who turned it into an anthem.

To Patrick Hughes for putting the pieces together.

To a cast and crew who made a film on faith.

And to the memories of my son Zaki and brother David, who live for eternity in the light of our Lord.

MOVIE CULTURE

You know, I'm a simple guy. I enjoy watching movies, when I get the chance, especially those that are inspirational. There is nothing better than a movie that leaves you uplifted; the type of film where everyone is talking about it afterwards, and discussing how it affected them.

But, hey, what do I know? I'm a radio and television personality. My focus is on politics, terrorism, and the future of America. The Hollywood film industry is a completely separate field from my news and political world, but every once in a while the two actually intersect. Take the few occasions when I can interview a Hollywood celebrity on my show; those brave enough to talk to a conservative, of course. I deal in truth and reality, while most of the Hollywood crowd lives on Fantasy Island.

Kevin Sorbo is one of those exceptions, and he has never been accused of fearing the truth. He's a no-nonsense, guy's-guy, straightforward and honest. The first time he joined me on my show, we hit it off. Over his visits to my studios, Kevin and I developed a friendship and mutual respect for one another.

I saw *God's Not Dead*, and it was a truly powerful film. Kevin's role in the movie played a large part in that. It was an emotionally impactful story where the audience left the theater feeling challenged and uplifted.

I called Kevin to congratulate him on the great success of the movie, and I said to him, "If you ever get a project that is interesting, something contemporary, that will inspire people, give me a call." I wanted to be a part of something that was positive and gave people hope again. Little did I know then that his wife had just conceived an idea she was planning to write with Dan Gordon, called *Let There Be Light.*

Kevin called me back a month later and we arranged to meet at my office in New York City.

What was I getting myself into? It's one thing to say you might be interested in funding a movie project, but honestly, only crazy people get into the film industry! By most accounts, it's a corrupt, slimy business. We've all read the papers, seen the lawsuits.

Still...movies can have a powerful effect on culture, and I had an honest desire to contribute to that intangible force. There is something valuable that happens when a good film impacts hearts and minds, and when a message resonates. The idea of participating in this production became something I really wanted to do, even though my skepticism about this new venture made me cautious.

Kevin came into my office first. Dan and Sam followed, and Kevin introduced Dan, who was clearly their designated storyteller. Normally the talkative one, I just sat still, listening to Dan. Our meeting lasted a full half hour, and by its conclusion, I was sold. From Dan, I had heard about a movie that I wanted to see. The plot and story convinced me, so my gut said "go," while my business brain said "wait!"

Against all my better, rational judgment, we had a hand-shake deal when they left my office. To say I was conflicted doesn't put it in the right light. I'm a decisive person, and I committed to the idea behind the project as much as to the film itself. I knew it was a roll of the dice. I felt like I would be part of something big, all the while recognizing it could go south in a moment.

As they began their search for the location of the shoot, they kept me apprised, but I didn't want to meddle. What did I know about producing a dramatic movie? I gave them my trust and left them alone.

The team started shooting in August, in Birmingham.

The script called for me to play a small role in the movie, as myself. That's a stretch! We scheduled them to film in New York at the very end of the month. My two scenes could be shot in one day, and so we scheduled the office scene for the morning, and then the broadcasting scene for right after I finished my television show that night.

I showed up at the office set, which was on a high floor in the Fox building in New York, and everything was ready to go. The place was abuzz with their crew moving equipment, testing microphones...I said to Kevin, "Look, I'm not the memory guru, here, so bear with me..."

He was his typical affable self. "Don't sweat it. We'll keep it loose. Remember, it's not live television! There's always another take."

That was an understatement. There were so many people around, and the space was a bit cramped in the office suite, which was a long ascetic hallway with some individual offices off it. One had been transformed into the hair and makeup room. The outer reception area, where the hallway ended, was crammed with equipment and technical experts. The sound cart was there, and the video guys had set up camp. The final door at the end of the suite gave into a white office that had been transformed into "my" space, one windowed wall with a high city view, some framed show posters and a conference table.

I walked in with Kevin and Sam to rehearse. Kevin made some joke about shooting the rehearsal. Apparently sometimes, as an actor, you do your best work in the rehearsal!

We shot the same scene about twenty times, because we had to do each take twice. I realized why I never became an actor (among many other reasons): I don't have the patience!

I will say this: The thing that blew me away that day was Sam's talent. At one point during the film, her character Katy is going through some intense stuff, and when I offer to provide publicity for the app that she and Sol are designing, she tears up—real tears! I was stunned. I'm not someone who cries, certainly not on cue. And what I found most poignant about her crying wasn't just the tears; it was that I believed her. It wasn't some trick, to just cry on cue. Each time we ran the scene, she became truly emotional. Until today, I still don't know how she did that.

Shortly after the election of Donald Trump, I received an email from Kevin. "Hey, Sean, we have the movie completed in a rough form, and we'd love to come to New York and do a screening for you. How can we set that up to best fit into your schedule?"

My emails tend more toward "brief." I sent back, "Send a screener, please. Just prefer to watch alone, thanks."

They provided a link for me.

It was with intense trepidation that I sat down, alone in my office, to watch the screener. Now, here's the weird part I knew what was going to happen in the movie. I had read the script, of course, so none of it was surprising, and yet...

There are so many twists and turns in this movie. I couldn't turn away. It's an emotional roller coaster. And this is, for me, the test of a great movie: It stayed with me. I kept thinking about it. The next day, I showed it to some friends and watched it again. I wrote the gang this:

Ok I watched the entire movie beginning to end. This is always something I need to do alone, just how I roll. To say that I am blown away is an understatement.

Like I wrote at the beginning of this story, I am a simple man. I set out with a goal to be part of a production that would affect people in a positive way. I am so proud to be involved in this movie, and for the opportunity to work with these gifted individuals. If this movie brings *light* to just one person, it has been successful. But I believe it will provide a light for each person who sees it.

SEAN HANNITY
May 2017

PREFACE

"Faith film" is an interesting phrase. In the motion picture business, it has a definite meaning. It is a film intended for a niche audience—people of faith. And the faith for which it is specifically intended is Christianity; the audience is its adherents.

There are times when it's a fairly crass term. It's intended to calculate a more-or-less guaranteed return if the target audience is reached.

But there's another kind of faith film, and sometimes, the two coincide. It is the kind of film not only intended for a faith audience but a film literally made *by* faith.

Let There Be Light is exactly such a film.

To start with, there was not only never really a chance of seeing it get made, there wasn't even a unanimous intent on getting it made.

I've been a screenwriter for longer than I care to admit. In May of this year, I will mark my fiftieth year in the biz, as they say. I have always been a studio writer and have written such films as *The Hurricane*, with Denzel Washington; *Wyatt Earp*, with Kevin Costner; *Passenger 57*, with Wesley Snipes; and *Murder in the First*, with Kevin Bacon. *Let There Be Light* marks my seventeenth feature-length film. I have also done around two to three hundred hours of network, cable, and premium cable television along the way, starting out as head writer of Michael Landon's *Highway to Heaven* on NBC over thirty years ago.

In each and every case, absolutely without exception, either I had an idea for a movie and pitched it to a studio, independent producers, or a television network or someone contacted my agent and said, "We've just optioned a book or the subject of a life story and think Dan Gordon might be right for this."

I was one of a shortlist of writers; I put together my "take" on the subject, then went to the studio and pitched my idea. I basically auditioned for every job I got, one way or the other.

Those are the only two ways it works in Hollywood. Or, at least, those are the only two ways it's ever worked in my career.

That is, up until *Let There Be Light*.

From the beginning, *Let There Be Light* fit no mold and proceeded according to neither my plan nor that of any studio or network, but, I firmly believe, according to God's plan. That's an awfully arrogant statement to make, I know, but since I've spent my life as a storyteller, let me tell you a story.

One day, I received a call from Sam Sorbo, wife of Kevin Sorbo. A mutual friend had introduced us and I found them to be a lovely couple. We flirted with a television series idea or two. As I recall, we even pitched one of them. And, as is the case with more than ninety percent of all the projects I've ever been involved with, absolutely nothing came of it.

Actually, that's not true.

A deep friendship that I have come to treasure came of it. But that doesn't pay the rent, keep the lights on, or get a film made. And that kind of friendship, many times, crashes on the rocks of the pressures of actually making a movie.

But, from the get-go, this one was different.

So, I get a call from Sam Sorbo. She says, "Would you be interested in writing a screenplay with me?"

"No."

"How come?"

"Because I don't write with other people. And in kindergarten, I never shared my toys or played well with others."

"Well, would you consider meeting with me for coffee?"

"No."

"How come?"

"I don't drink coffee."

"Tea?"

"Don't drink tea. But I'll meet you, and I'll bring a bottle of water. You can drink what you like."

I met her at a shopping mall in Calabasas, and she told me a story. A really good story that got my attention immediately, so I said, "Okay. Here's what I'll consider doing. There's something in this. You write the first draft and then give it to me, and I get to do what I want. Then, we'll both look at it and see if we think it's a movie."

"Deal," Sam answered with a smile.

Incredibly, at almost exactly the same time we were meeting and Sam commenced writing the screenplay, Sean Hannity called Kevin Sorbo, who had appeared on Hannity's show on Fox News a few times, plugging *God's Not Dead* and his other faith-based films. And Sean says, "If you ever have a faith-based movie that you think I might be interested in, bring it to me, because I think movies can do more than anything else to influence culture, and that's something I'd be interested in."

Now, may I say, that's just plain goofy. The money never chases you. You ALWAYS chase the money and, usually, you run out of breath before it does. But here was one of the most well-known television personalities in the entire world saying, "If you've got something, I'd be interested in financing it."

Of course, we didn't have something. All we had was the story that Sam and I had agreed to write—the one we had not yet written.

So, the three of us flew to New York and we pitched Sean in his office at Fox News. Now, outside of the president of the United States and a one-armed paper hanger, there is probably no person on Earth busier than Sean Hannity. He doesn't have a lot of time, and he doesn't like to spend a lot of time just talking. He is a very dynamic doer. We basically had twenty minutes to a half hour between his three-hour radio show and his one-hour nightly television show to pitch him the story of a screenplay which didn't exist.

But it was a heck of a story.

Its genesis was in Sam's pure heart, and for me, it was probably one of the most personal stories I've ever done. It deals with the death of a much-loved firstborn child. It contains the heartbreaking bitterness of two people who once loved each other and who have been torn apart by loss. It deals with lacking faith, and finding faith. It delves deep into the hours I have known of PTSD, of washing down pain pills with vodka and still feeling the pain. Of what F. Scott Fitzgerald called the "real dark night of the soul," where "it is always three o'clock in the morning, day after day."

On those nights, after a rather nasty car accident that tore my rotator cuff, fractured a collar bone, and triggered some horrific memories of both my son's fatal car accident and wars in which I've participated, I would sit, zonked out in a chair, since I could not sleep lying down for three months, blitzed out of my mind, watching infomercials. And the next day, to my amazement, I would find I had ordered six cases of whatever the previous night's huckster had been selling.

The story contains a combination of the purity of Sam's soul and a few hard-won truths. It also contains the story of a pal of mine who used to be a mobbed-up wiseguy and who found Christ in solitary confinement during the time he was euphemistically residing in government housing. It makes a heck of a story. And I managed to tell it before Sean had to go on the air for his radio show or start prepping his nightly television program.

There are a lot of indecisive people on Earth—a lot of people who do not follow the truth of their own convictions and even more who have no convictions to follow. Sean Hannity fits into none of those categories. He said okay on the spot.

He asked what the budget was, and we told him.

He simply said, "Okay." Just like that.

He then said, with the hard glint in his eye of an Irish construction worker, "Don't come back to me for a penny more because you're over budget."

And, as easy as that, we were in business.

Without our realizing it, the Big G was orchestrating everything all along. People came to be a part of our film, not just because it was another gig, but because it was their heart-wrenching story as well.

Our story touches upon cancer because my brother died in my arms of a brain tumor. And as he did, his last words were about what he was, apparently, catching a glimpse of. "It's so beautiful," he said. "It's so beautiful!" I had never seen a smile like that before on his face.

A young actress, who was to play a pivotal role in the film, auditioned for us. But it wasn't just a gig for her, because despite her youth, she was a cancer survivor, and this was her story as much as ours.

Another young woman who turned in a magnificent performance had to be done by a certain hour because she needed eight hours of dialysis. It was her faith that kept her going, and she poured every ounce of hers into it.

Our producer/line producer was nothing less than a Jedi warrior. He made miracles happen on the set. Usually, you search for locations. Our locations searched for us, and found us.

Every step of the way, through every crisis, the Big G made it better, and there was always a lesson for all of us to learn.

Sam stepped up with an idea, and she carried it across the finish line...on faith.

Kevin had to carry the load of starring and directing, and he did them both...on faith.

And Sean Hannity was the best boss anyone could ask for. He left us completely alone. He never visited the set, never even called. He just said, "Bring me back a good movie." And he did it...on faith.

The end result is a film that makes audiences laugh, cry, and stand up and cheer, and, I do believe, renews in them that most precious of all commodities—faith.

Let There Be Light is, you might say, a faith film.

DAN GORDON
April 2017

CHAPTER 1

Sol Harkens thought of himself as the Muhammad Ali of atheist debaters. He dispatched Christian apologists with the speed and style and grace of a man used to using words the way the great Ali used footwork and a left jab. He wasn't so much a debater as he was a pugilist, a matador, a great fencer, or a Shaolin Kung Fu master. He not only floated like a butterfly and stung like a bee, he could cut off a verbal opponent at the knees with a well-placed, sidelong glance, with a charming wink and a nod to an audience he held in the palm of his hand. He was Wyatt Earp at the O.K. Corral. He fancied himself Babe Ruth pointing into the center field stands and promising the pitcher, with a mocking grin, that whatever he had to throw at him, Sol would literally knock the next one out of the park. He was a behind-the-back, Magic Johnson pass, a Michael Jordan slam dunk, the camera following in slow-mo, the turn-around jump-shot, his generation's hero thrown up on the pop charts; he was the bomb in the baby carriage, wired to the radio. Lethal. Deadly. He was the Ferrari to the Christian apologist's Fiat 500. The D'Artagnan of dogma. At six foot three and a trim 210 pounds and, he thought to himself, devastatingly handsome, he was the complete package. And he knew it.

He warmed up for debates not with flashcards, but with shadowboxing. In the land of the blind, where even a one-eyed man was king, he had telescopic vision. He had single-handedly turned religious debate into blood sport. He didn't defeat his opponents, he body slammed them and, quite frankly, he didn't care what it took to do it—intellect, emotions, sarcasm, or even, though he would never admit it to himself, the carefully crafted pimping out of his own personal tragedy, the death of his eight-year-old son. He felt neither shame nor embarrassment. Nor was he bothered by a hint of someone else's sense of morality. He was like Han Solo, shooting Greedo under the table. He liked that image of himself—the intellectual as dashing pirate privateer, or gunslinger, or the aforementioned most flamboyant, charismatic, and, quite possibly, greatest heavyweight champion of all time, Muhammad Ali.

Sol had his own set of groupies to whom he threw the occasional crumb of witticism or wink, and a seemingly endless supply of Russian supermodels who were happy to trade the pleasure of their company for the rubbed-off glory of being on the arm of the darling of the New York glitz and literati scene.

Bill Maher, he thought, could be his Mini-Me, and he chuckled heartily at his own witticism and the mere thought of balancing Maher in the palm of his hand while trading verbal blows with the ghost of a younger Billy Graham.

How he wished there was someone on the other side with his own intellectual capacity and good looks.

He and Billy Graham.

Now, *that* would have been a debate. *That* would have been an adversary worthy of his prowess and charisma.

Instead, he was up against what he could only regard as a plodding, pedestrian Christian apologist.

If he was the Harlem Globetrotters, then Dr. Reinhardt Fournier was the Washington Generals. The man was a walking footstool, his only purpose in life to make Harkens look good by comparison.

And not just good, Harkens thought. *Fan-freaking-tastic.*

The New Union College Auditorium, scene of some of the greatest debates in New York of the past hundred years, was packed to its ornate rafters. New Yorkers had come to regard a Sol Harkens debate with the same sense of bloodlust with which the Pamplonans regarded the first bloodletting in the running of the bulls.

Harkens had been the baby of the group of all the gang down at Elaine's.

He had hobnobbed with Plimpton and Mailer, Talese and Christopher Hitchens. Woody Allen, who almost never looked up from his meal, would accord Harkens a nod. When Elaine's closed down and Woody began playing Dixieland at the Carlyle instead, Harkens made it a habit to drop in at least once a month. On at least one occasion, he wrote on a slip of paper his request that Woody and company play that great Dixieland classic, *"Bur-GUHN-dy Blues Street."* This afforded Woody the opportunity to play the George Lewis clarinet solo, which he ended with an appreciative nod toward Sol's table and endeared Sol even more to the Russian supermodel of the month.

Afterward, he would drop in to the piano bar midway between the showroom and the restaurant of the Carlyle, and sit in with Earl, the last of the great piano bar pianists in the Big Apple. For Harkens was no mean player in his own right.

In addition, he was a regular at Le Veau d'Or on 60th and Lex, where he would invariably be greeted with kisses on both cheeks by Cathy, the beautiful owner, who kept his table waiting—fourth one on the right from the entrance—for whenever he chose to arrive. She would stop at his table and trade *bon mots* and the news of the day, as she would with the still-dapper Mr. Talese and the very dashing Charlie Whittingham, former publisher of some of the greatest magazines of the twentieth century who, at six foot five with a patch over one eye and a shock of white hair, resembled nothing so much as a distinguished, intellectual John Wayne and always exchanged felicitations with Sol and whatever beauty of the moment was on his arm. Usually, after a dinner of coq au vin or seared turbot with pommes frites and a crisp rosé, Sol would stroll down 60th to Harry Cipriani's for a late-night Bellini, exchanging pleasantries with Ricardo, the maître d', in Italian, before cabbing it back to his brownstone.

Life was, to all appearances, absolutely grand for Sol Harkens. It was only when he was ensconced in his loft on the top story of the brownstone that things got a little bit darker. That's when he needed the vodka and handfuls of diazepam to go to sleep.

But sleep never came, only late-night infomercials—Wipe-Wowies and Miracle Mops, OxyToxyClean and Miracle Rubber Boat Sealer ads. Finally, he would pass out on his couch somewhere before sunup, and arise, vampire-like, somewhere around noon, pop an upper, take the red out of his eyes with enough Visine to float a battleship, and go out to face yet another day.

Doctor Harkens was mulling over all of his attributes, assets, and deficits, the flotsam and jetsam of what, on the surface, appeared to be a glamorous life and was, in reality, shadowboxing in the dark with ghosts of tragedies that never receded completely into the past but clung to him like a desperate lover or some kind of mold.

It was at that point that he became aware of Fournier droning on from the podium across the stage. Harkens would let him talk as long as he wanted. It was intellectual rope-a-dope, and Fournier plunged in, not without gusto and a certain sense of his own importance.

"The problem," began the Reverend Dr. Fournier, a man of equal height and bearing to Sol Harkens but nowhere near the chiseled features and blow-dry cut of the man that swooning postgraduate students referred to as "the George Clooney of atheists."

"The problem," Fournier intoned again, "with those who would posit that inanimate matter somehow, through a great unexplained cosmic coincidence, morphed from dead to living entities, which then evolved *without* intelligent design but simply in a random fashion, into ballerinas and nuclear physicists, is that they always ignore the basic question." There was a gentlemanly Southern accent in his dulcet tones, a masculine, lisp-less, carefully-cultivated Capote-esque quality, a sort of Bill Buckley without the lizard tongue. "And the basic question is, 'Where did the inanimate matter come from? Who created it?' Because, being inanimate, it could not have created itself, no matter what Darwinian theory is applied," he said, looking directly at Harkens.

As if, Harkens thought to himself, *I would ever stoop to Darwinian Theory to score points off an intellectual slug like him.*

"No matter what Darwinian theory is applied," Dr. Fournier continued, with a seemingly nonchalant shrug of his shoulders, "and I emphasize the word 'theory,' absolutely none answers the question, 'What was there before there was no *there* there?'" He let that one hang as if he had mentioned something as original as eggs laid by tigers.

"And, parenthetically, if you subscribe to the theory that aliens from other galaxies came to our world and influenced in one way or another the creation of species, which by the way I personally neither accept nor discount, the question still remains, who created those alien beings? The God I worship is Lord of the Universe, not simply planet Earth, nor our solar system, nor this, that, nor any other galaxy, but Lord of ALL CREATION!" He stretched his arms out wide as if encompassing all creation itself. "And isn't it interesting," he continued, "that the story of Genesis is in no way contradicted by the theory of evolution. Rather, it explains creation in a way that ancient man as well as modern man can understand. God creates the heavens and the earth. He doesn't jump then to the creation of man. Instead, plants and vegetation are created, followed by living creatures of the sea. Then, birds are created and later livestock, the creatures that move along the ground, and finally, at the apex of creation, there is mankind!"

He gazed out into the audience, trying to establish eye contact with any seemingly friendly face. "How fascinating," he said, carefully enunciating every syllable, "that the Bible, this supposed collection of superstitions and fables, accurately delineates the so-called Darwinian progression of life from the sea to the land, finally supposedly evolving, without plan, design, or Creator, into mankind. If I were looking at the two theories, those of Creation and Darwinism, for the first time, I, as a rational being, would say it takes a greater leap of faith by far to accept the notion of inanimate particles, whose origins are unexplained, somehow becoming living entities, which, through a random process, produce Miley Cyrus!"

That was the zinger, Harkens thought. The phrase he had been building toward for the last ten minutes, and all he got was a chuckle from the odd New Yorker born-bgain Christians, who were hoping against hope that their champion could score a point against the great Sol Harkens.

But the audience, by and large, was made up of Bernie Sanders millennials.

Book posters on either side of the stage hawked the debaters' various tomes, *Aborting God: The Reasoned Choice* on one side and Fournier's flat-footed title, *A Return to Faith*, on the other.

Fascinating, Harkens thought to himself, *I've got a Bible-thumper who's appealing to reason, rather than emotion.* And thus, like an ambidextrous middleweight who, with lightning speed, could switch from right-hander to southpaw, Harkens made the instant choice to dump his prearranged and long ago prepackaged, logical dismantling of Christian doctrine in favor of enough snarky sarcasm to make Rachel Maddow look like a contemplative nun and some pure, raw, one might even say evangelical, emotion. If this bozo wanted to boogie with Harkens as an intellectual equal, Sol would lie back on the imaginary ropes, let him punch himself out, and then spring back as an evangelist of atheism. He was as much of a tent-show huckster as any snake-oil salesman, with one vital difference: Harkens believed, with his heart and soul and every fiber of his being, his own sales pitch.

Sol laid back and waited for his moment, and Fournier offered it up like a punched-out George Foreman telegraphing a wild left hook that left an opening through which a Mack Truck could maneuver.

"Now then," said Fournier, "the basic tenet of Christianity is—"

And that was the moment the Ali in Harkens danced off the ropes and restarted the fight, on his own terms.

"Whoa! I'm sorry! Bzzzt. Coach's time out!" Harkens said with his rakish grin, holding up the coach's "T" symbol in the seventh game of the NBA finals of his mind.

"I think I might at least be afforded the common courtesy of completing my opening statement," Fournier harrumphed, rather like Foghorn Leghorn saying, "Now, son! I think I might be afforded," etc.

The moderator, a pinch-nosed woman who spoke in a nasal New York twang not unlike a certain cable news reporter married to a former chairman of the Fed, intoned solemnly, "Dr. Harkens, the rules of the debate were agreed upon by both you and Dr. Fournier."

"And," said Sol, agreeably, "I believe the rules also included the topic of the debate, which was not, *quote*, The Basic Tenet of Christianity, *close quote*, but, *quote*, The Existence of God, *colon*, Harmless Belief, *comma*, Blessing, *comma*, or Curse, *question mark*, *close quote*. You're not up here speaking for Christians, which covers a pretty broad spectrum of yahoos. I mean, Episcopalians, Methodists, Lutherans, Seventh Day Adventists—whom I don't think your guys actually believe are completely kosher—Pentecostals, Baptists, throw in a snake charmer or two, some holy rollers, and the church, dare I say, of Christian, pardon the expression, Science, and you've got a pretty heavy load. Nay, you are too modest, sir. Nor are you here as an expert on Darwinism. You are here, my dear Doctor Fournier, speaking for the Father, the Great Bearded Watchmaker in the sky, the Big G, the Rock of Ages, Da Man Himself, let's give it up for Gawwwwd Alllllmighty!" The audience roared with laughter as Sol gave his best televangelist delivery, complete with finger pointing high. He looked at them and not at Fournier, rather like Jack Kennedy addressing the camera rather than the four-o'clock-shadowed, sweating, hair-matted-down, grey-suited pallor of Richard Nixon. "You want to debate that fairy tale you call Christianity? I'll boogie with you on that one all night long. But I came here not just for a little theological chitchat and some canapes but to sell books, namely my new tome, *Aborting God*. So why don't we just stick to the topic, what do you say, Doc? You speak for the Spirit in the Sky and I'll cheerlead for Sex, Drugs, and Rock and Roll."

The audience cheered.

They laughed.

They giggled like a plump baby being tickled under the armpits.

They belonged to Sol, and he knew it. They knew it. They knew he knew it, and each was loving every second of it.

"I have to take issue with that, Dr. Harkens."

"I kinda figured you would," Sol replied, coming out from behind his podium and leaning against it as if he were a vodka martini with a twist at Dukes Bar, employing a bit of a southwestern twang to which he had no right at all.

"Because," Fournier said, piously, "it is only as a Christian that I can approach God, the Father."

This isn't Ali-Foreman, thought Harkens, almost allowing himself to pity his Elmer Fudd-like opponent. *This is Ali-Quarry!*

"Those are your limitations, and none of my own. I can approach atheism from any direction: court jester, philosopher, a puppet, a pauper, a pirate, a poet, a pawn, or a king, to quote that other great religious leader, the late lamented Francis Albert the First," Sol said, genuflecting as elegantly as Sydney Greenstreet offered up a salaam in *Casablanca*.

"But," said Fournier, still holding out some vague hope of landing if not a knockout, at least a narrow win on points, "you still haven't answered my question. If there is no Creator, how, then, is there creation?"

"Once again," said Sol, totally ignoring his opponent and eyeing a semi-ravishing grad student in a rather form-fitting cardigan in the seventh row, center, "though I'm more than willing to have Chuckie Darwin's back on that one, *that* is not our topic. Our topic for this debate is whether the mythology to which you subscribe is blessing or curse. Can someone get Dr. Fournier a copy of the program, so he can see what we've been hyping?" Chuckles rippled up to him like water lapping at his toes. "At any rate, back to the subject at hand. Why, dear sir, should I believe in God any more than the tooth fairy, which, if you ask me, is a far more benign form of religious indoctrination. At least the tooth fairy coughs up a buck or two for every little canine she finds under my pillow. Your so-called GAWWWD consigns me to Hell for the crime of simply following the inclinations that supposedly He Himself has created within me. That, if you ask me, is rather like a cop planting a doobie in my pocket and then busting me for..." Sol took a hit off an imaginary joint, then exhaled the final word, "...possession."

"But, you make my point for me!"

"That, may I say, my dear reverend, will be the day."

The intrepid Fournier now sprung his own trap. "God gave us free will, the ability to choose between good and evil. That's man's choice, sir, your choice, not God's!"

"Ah, yes, God's gift of free will that comes with the promise of eternal damnation, fire, and brimstone. Your supposed gift of free will is to be exercised only at spiritual gunpoint, making

God nothing more than the Great Carjacker in the Sky. 'You got the free will to give me your keys, Jack, or I'll bust a cap in your head and send you to hell!'" said Harkens, with a passable *Boyz n' Tha Hood* line rendering.

"Free will," sounded Fournier, believing he was springing his trap, "means, sir, you choose not only the action but the consequence!"

"Odd, sir," Harkens replied. "That's exactly what ISIS says. 'You can convert or die.' Let me ask you something: Is the God you believe in any different than the God of ISIS? They certainly don't think so. They're no less sincere in their beliefs than you are in yours. As for me, I think you're both smoking the same dope. The only difference is, yours is in a joint and theirs is in a hookah. But the result is always the same—people killed in the name of Christ, Yahweh, or Allah! That's the gift of your belief in the Divine Creator. Well, I say, you keep it, Reverend. I don't need the pablum. Nor does anybody else. Look at what ISIS does, and all of it not in the name of atheism but in the name of God! You honestly believe we need more of that?"

Now it was Fournier's turn to taste the ropes on his back, as Sol landed punches at will.

"I can't speak for ISIS," said the aptly named apologist. "I can only speak as a Christian."

"All right," said Sol, dancing away onstage in a kind of combination of Muhammad Ali, Michael Jackson, and Mick Jagger. "I'm feeling magnanimous. You want to change the rules of the debate because you've already lost the argument we're supposed to be debating in favor of the one you WISH we were debating? Have at it. Give me your best shot. I'm lyin' on the ropes, just like Ali." He held up his arms like Ali blocking shots, and then peeked around with an impish grin as the audience lapped it all up like puppies going for kibble.

"Christianity," began Fournier, realizing he may already have lost the audience to his opponent but valiantly struggling to maintain his evangelistic focus. *If you only save one soul...*"Christianity offers forgiveness as its basic tenet, to get back to my original statement, which you so artfully distorted."

"Does it indeed?"

"Absolutely! *John 3:16*: 'For God so loved the world that he gave his only begotten Son, that whosoever believeth in him should NOT perish, but have everlasting life!'"

Harkens mouthed the words of *John 3:16* along with Fournier, mockingly. But it wasn't just theatrics. This was the part of the debate he knew was coming, the part in which he could actually use honesty as his most deceptive weapon.

"That," continued Fournier, unable to suppress the rising defiance in his voice, "is the loving and compassionate God I know and love and serve."

"Well, this is where we leave the realm of theory and get personal, pal."

As if to emphasize the point, Sol stepped away from the podium to the apron of the stage and sat down, dangled his feet over the edge, looked the audience directly in the eyes, and spoke so softly that the audience craned their necks, listening like lovers hanging on every word. This was where baring his soul, speaking as honestly and as nakedly as he could, became Sol's best and, yes, well-rehearsed weapon, none of which made it any less true, nor any less painful.

"Because," he continued, "I had a beautiful, perfect, glorious son, who, I guarantee you, I loved as much as your supposed deity loved his 'begotten son.' And my 'begotten son' got a rather nasty form of cancer, which I watched eat away at his helpless, tiny body and ultimately kill him before he reached his ninth birthday."

Sol got up from his perch and knelt on the stage, palms together as if in supplication in a piety he would have embraced if only it could have delivered that which he had longed for most.

Reverend Dr. Fournier, for his part, struggled to maintain his composure. This was truly beyond the pale, pulling out the personal tragedy as a trump card. How would he counter the sympathy vote? He chided himself for his own callousness. *Consider the man,* he thought to himself, and then immediately discarded the thought as futile. If there was a soul for saving in this room, clearly it would not be the implacable, obstinate, and bitter one locked in Sol Harkens.

"Now, if I were a praying man, I'd pray to see my son just one more time, but then that would mean praying to the very so-called God that killed him!"

Sol very slowly got to his feet, turning his back to the audience for just an instant, so that he could, with a flare of theatricality, turn back toward them.

"So, rather than being vindictive, I'm willing to say, my son's death was just plain bad luck, a quirk of genetics, a bad roll of the cosmic dice, or maybe some corporate villain who poisoned the water—I'll even entertain that bit of proletarian class warfare if you like. And with the help of some fairly effective chemicals and a healthy dollop of vodka, I can somehow make it through the night without blowing my brains out." And here, Sol pantomimed doing exactly that, pretending to fire a gun into his all-too-real brain that allowed him no rest, no respite, no moment's reprieve from the pain of the death of his firstborn son. He allowed himself to feel that, sucked it up, and then continued, allowing the bitterness to turn to bile, bile to anger, and the anger into righteous rage.

"Because I accept that's just the luck of the draw. But don't you dare tell me about the love and compassion of your so-called God. Because if he felt like sacrificing his only begotten son, that's his business, but he should have bloody well kept his hands off of mine!"

He brought his hand down like a thunderclap against the podium, and the audience burst into applause. They were an audience no more; he was ready to turn them into a lynch mob.

"In the Old Testament, the punishment for violating the Sabbath was death by stoning. The Inquisition and the Crusades killed millions in the name of Christ, and ISIS does it today in the name of Allah."

Suddenly, with an alacrity that surprised even the reverend himself, Fournier sling-shotted back off the ropes, to continue the metaphor. "That number, so often quoted by atheists, is simply not true! And most of the world's wars have nothing to do with religion at all!"

"Really? That would certainly come as a shock to the guys who slammed into the Twin Towers saying '*Allahu Akbar*'! Is that a phrase that you'd be uncomfortable with, 'God is great'? What do you think the 'Lord of Hosts' means? It means the God of Armies! But just to indulge you, I'll grant you that point, and put it another way, one that even you can understand. Nobody ever committed genocide in the name of sex, drugs, and rock and roll. All they ever did was party! And if you can't see that humanity is better off with that than the myths you peddle, which have caused nothing but misery for thousands of years, then, pardon the pun, but God have mercy on your soul. As for me, I have nothing but pity and disdain. You want to know what my religious credo is? 'Party on, Wayne!' In the face of death, 'Party on, Garth!' Instead of war, 'Party on!' Instead of damnation, 'Party on!' Instead of Judgement Day, I'll take a snow day and 'Party on!'"

The audience was on their feet, cheering, but Sol wasn't ready to let go of them. They weren't yet at the frenzy he was looking for. This was the *coup de grâce*, the moment at which he would impale the bull on his sword, the moment he would bury this pious huckster and then spit on his grave.

"Don't look for any meaning in life," he shouted, "because there isn't any! No purpose, no rhyme nor reason! You don't need God to be moral. You don't need a deity to know it's not cool to cut somebody's head off or burn them alive or sell their children into slavery, especially not in the *name* of that supposed deity! All you need—" he pointed to the crowd "all *you* need, all *you* need, all *you* need IS YOUR HUMANITY!" He ended with arms stretched out wide, mocking Fournier's supposed savior on the cross, as the audience stood, applauding wildly, cheering, whistling, shouting out the atheist equivalent of "hosanna."

Reverend Fournier, sensing utter defeat, simply did the mental equivalent of shrugging his shoulders and shaking his head. He would not give Harkens the compliment of his anger, so he stifled it and sent a quick prayer to Heaven, asking God to grant him patience and peace.

Superstar Sol had so totally destroyed his adversary that to stick around and sign books would have damaged the drama of the moment. And so, he simply stalked off stage, throwing a look over his shoulder toward his adoring fans.

My books are pre-autographed. They're for sale over there. As for me, I'm going to snuggle up to a bottle of liquid comfort and boogie!

He walked straight into the wings, out the stage door into his waiting Benz, and roared off into the Manhattan skyline, leaving poor Fournier alone on the stage to wonder how, exactly, he could get off with some remnant of dignity intact.

CHAPTER 2

Sol Harkens's apartment was a shrine, not surprisingly, to Sol Harkens.

It was the quintessential hipster New York loft in a trendy West Village neighborhood full of eateries and assorted latte and juice bars. Here and there were falafel joints that hid behind the title of "Mediterranean Cuisine," especially after the 2014 Israel-Hamas war that triggered protests in front of Meir's Falafel, during which signs reading DAMN YOUR RACIST HUMMUS; SPREAD HUMMUS, NOT HATE; and NO FASCIST FALAFEL FOR ME sprang up like mushrooms after a spring rain. That's when Meir's Falafel became Mario's Mediterranean Cuisine.

Sol was an habitué of all of them, well known—indeed, a local celebrity of sorts—and his picture graced the walls of those eateries, which, whether he admitted it or not, was not a small part of their attraction for him.

He was close enough to the Village, where he could still score with an impressionable grad student, and he wasn't that far from the Brooklyn Bridge, which he still loved to walk across and, from Dumbo at the other side of the river, look at the unendingly beautiful but, since 9/11, heart-achingly somber skyline of lower Manhattan. It was a sight of which he never tired, but it had been a while since he had seen it.

For some reason, the passing of time since his oldest boy's death and his younger sons' coming of age, since a seemingly endless stream of relationships—none of which lasted longer than three months and most of which were measured in days instead of weeks—instilled in him its own kind of growing melancholy, a kind of personal PTSD, in which he felt safe only within the confines of the multi-million-dollar shrine to his own intellect, which, he supposed, at the end of the day, was the only thing that could never betray him.

This ongoing self-pity was only magnified by the walls lined with posters of every one of his books, which included such titles as, *There's No There, There*; *The God Virus*; and his newly minted hit and personal favorite, *Aborting God: The Reasoned Choice*. They were blown up to look like previews of coming attractions, with sales figures splashed across the bottoms as if to validate the importance of each tome. Wherever he looked, he saw a picture of himself; the chiseled features, the blow-dried cut, the honest sadness that had taken ahold of his eyes and then given his intellectual's visage a kind of gravitas, which had replaced the boy wonder he had once been.

He had a professional chef's kitchen, which he never used for anything but the countertop. Like almost all New Yorkers, he ordered out for everything but coffee and the croissants he bought at François down the street.

There was the Steinway baby grand, which he no longer played.

There was the full bar in the corner, next to the exposed, used-brick wall, of which he made more than ample use.

There were the deep-cushioned, beautiful leather sofas that faced the big-screen TV, which was never off, as the voices of the talking-head commentators provided his only ongoing companionship. But he could only take them for so long.

By ten, he had usually consumed half a bottle of vodka and switched from Rachel Maddow to watching TMZ. He was numb enough to make no sense at all of the ongoing dramas of pierced pop singers, wife-abusing athletes, C-list celebs spotted staggering out of SUVs in front of the latest velvet-roped den of iniquity, overdosed rappers whose relatives fought like vultures for the rights to the estate, or the bottom-feeding sycophants who regarded each human tragedy as another one-liner. And then there were the ample-bottomed, semi-beautiful sisters of no apparent talent whatsoever, who were famous only for the fact that they were famous, an unending soap opera of human frailties and failings in which Sol somehow found comfort that he was not counted amongst them. No matter how much he drank or how many pills he popped, there were those to whom he could feel superior. That feeling usually lasted until around one o'clock in the morning, with the realization that the only reason he was not on the TMZ paparazzi parade was that, absent his untimely death, he was, quite simply, too old for it. These were all kids, twenty-somethings in the very center of a parade that he felt, more and more, was passing him by.

By two o'clock, he was washing diazepams down with the vodka and no longer bothering with the twist of lemon.

By three o'clock, the bottle was typically empty and sleep was still avoiding him, and he was reduced to watching late-night carnival barkers selling the odd knickknacks of capitalism, which he ordered with the fervor of a penitent rushing to the cross and whose purchase he completely forgot about by noon the next day when he arose.

Thus, every day produced a kind of surprise. One day, there were six cases of Wipe-Wowies. Another day, close to a dozen

Miracle Mops. There were cleaning fluids and rubberized seal-
ers, gadgets with twenty different tools all-in-one, Japanese
sushi knives, gym equipment he never unpacked, and miracle
wrinkle cream usually ordered by women of a certain age but
to whose charms he had succumbed, he knew not when. There
were hands-free binoculars, two pairs of sauna pants, three
cans of bald-spot miracle spray paint, the incredible shrinking
miracle garden hose, which was odd, in that Sol lived in a loft
without so much as a potted plant, and the *pièce de résistance*,
a Potty-Putter, which allowed one to perfect one's putts with a
miniature green and sawed-off putter whilst ensconced upon
the porcelain throne.

Sol Harkens sat in front of the pre-dawn glow of the fifty-
inch electronic oracle, which promised happiness for three
easy payments of $39.95, *shipping-and-handling-not-included*,
as he sucked his vodka, swallowed his Valium, and gazed about
him and muttered to no one in particular, "Livin' the dream."

Within forty-eight hours, he would receive a device that
cooked eggs into limpid, cylindrical shapes of no obvious
point or reason.

It would be the highlight of his day.

CHAPTER 3

Sol drove his souped-up, four-seater Benz along a winding, picture-postcard-perfect, Norman Rockwell Connecticut country road, which wound its way past quaint, slat-board farmhouses dating back to the Revolutionary War; a monastery for cloistered, contemplative nuns; a thoroughbred horse farm, and, finally, opened up into the tiny suburban community where he had spent the early years of his now-dissolved marriage to his incongruously Christian wife, Katy, and their two remaining boys, Connor and Gus.

Though he hated to admit it, even to himself, he felt a twinge every time he pulled up to that house. Despite the unspeakable tragedy of the catastrophic illness and subsequent death of his eight-year-old child, and the rancor of his divorce, if forced into a moment of honesty or if faced with his own drunken reflection in a 4:00 a.m. mirror, Sol would have been compelled to admit to himself that, in addition to the sadness and bitterness, this home was the place where he had once spent the happiest days of his life.

He and Katy had not yet been married a year when their boy Davey was born. And, being a writer, Sol's office was in his home, in the room now occupied by his fourteen-going-on-forty-year-old son, Gus.

In those days, Sol wrote from the early morning hours, as opposed to the vampire-like writing habits of the past several years. He would begin his writing days at six in the morning so that he could knock off at two and enjoy a late lunch with his beautiful wife and smiling infant son. Then, in the long, late afternoons of summer, somewhere between four thirty and six, as shadows stretched across the lawn, they would lay out on a blanket in the backyard with slices of watermelon and tall, cold glasses of homemade lemonade and watch their child progress from giggling infant to toddler, marking each event with the joyful enthusiasm known only to first-time parents. There was the first time Davey had rolled over, the first time he had begun to crawl...backwards, the first time he had grasped the notion of forward momentum, and the miraculous first time he had stood, on wobbling legs, his tiny hands wrapped around his father's fingers, smiling and laughing as if he had just conquered the world.

He would squeal with delight as Sol tossed him up into the air, caught him, and brought him back in toward his chest, the sweet baby smell and softness of his child's skin brushing up against his cheek. His wife was beautiful and radiant, wearing motherhood in all her glory, and life itself had never seemed so unbelievably simple and joyous. If their baby laughed, they both laughed with him. Everything he did was miraculous. Every smile, giggle, full-throated belly laugh, each new accomplishment, became the highlight of every day. Each of them knew, for the first time, the limitless love that parents feel for their firstborn child.

He always remembered a passage as he pulled into the driveway of that once happiest of all homes. It was from *David Copperfield*, when Dickens's young hero recalls his mother and infant sibling. Sol had once, in a drunken, maudlin moment, memorized it, and sometimes in the early morning, alcoholic hours, he recited it to himself, and was always surprised at the tears he felt streaming down his face.

"I spoke to her, and she started, and cried out. But seeing me, she called me her Davy, her own boy! And coming half across the room to meet me, kneeled down upon the ground and kissed me, and laid my head down on her bosom near the little creature that was nestling there, and put its hand up to my lips.

I wish I had died. I wish I had died then, with that feeling in my heart! I should have been more fit for heaven than I ever have been since.

'He is your brother,' said my mother, fondling me. 'Davy, my pretty boy. My poor child.'

Davey was what Sol and Katy had named their child, after Dickens's sweetest of all literary creations.

"Davey," Sol would whisper to no one in the darkness of drunken, dark nights of the soul, "Davey, my pretty boy. My poor child."

But, of course, he had not died then, and he did not believe in Heaven; neither then nor, especially, now. He believed, in fact, in nothing. He was simply filling out time. *No*, he thought to himself, *I'm killing time, while earnestly waiting for it to kill me…and of course*, he thought, *paying alimony.*

The joy of this home had long since morphed into nothing but a support payment. It was money he could have spent on himself and his latest Russian supermodel girlfriend in Turks and Caicos or perhaps a baronial villa in Puglia. Instead, he coughed up alimony and child support in the tens of thousands of dollars per month. That was the price that came with literary financial success. They had a computer program that punched in your income. It was called the Disso-mat. It computed the number of years you had been married, the number of children you had, their ages, and the costs of their private schools, and spat out a number. There was nothing on which Sol spent more, he thought bitterly, and nothing for which he got less. *The divorce courts turn you into an ATM. The Disso-mat*, he thought, with the kind of self-pity he usually reserved for Enzo, the bartender at Harry Cipriani in Manhattan, whose real name was Achmed and who was Egyptian instead of Italian, and who offered up the requisite sympathetic ear of his profession and commiserated with Sol Harkens's predicament in both Arabic and a markedly Sicilian dialect.

If it weren't for the alimony and the child support, he could be driving a Lamborghini instead of the Benz.

Thus, he honked the horn, hoping his boys would appear for their every-other-weekend visit without necessitating the unpleasantness that always flowed from each meeting, no matter how innocuous, with his now ex-wife.

He honked again, but again, there was no answer. The boys, he knew, were probably in the back of the house, their ears plugged into headsets, or perhaps they were in the backyard shooting hoops. *But Katy would have heard*, Sol thought, as he gritted his teeth at the unending loop of thoughts that began, always, with Katy, and ended, always, with thoughts of alimony and child support.

She would have heard the horn and ignored it. It would have been to her a personal affront, a lack of decency, and thus, the test of wills began always anew, even before they set eyes upon one another.

He could honk again, but what would be the use? Round one, she wins on points. He was bloodied, but unbowed.

He thought of calling the boys' cell phones but sucked it up, opened the door, and slammed it shut behind him with that resounding, self-satisfying Germanic thud, and walked up to the front door with all the joy of a condemned and shackled man, hand and foot, ascending the gallows.

He rang the bell and pulled his six-hundred-and-fifty-dollar pair of shades off his forehead and down into place, masking his eyes like a tournament poker player looking for any advantage he could get.

He heard her footsteps across the hardwood floors.

Each knew every detail so intimately about the other. He knew she would be barefoot. She knew he would be wearing the shades.

He heard the tumblers in the lock of the door, to which he no longer possessed a key.

It opened and there she stood, still annoyingly beautiful... and barefoot.

"Hey," she said, with almost the smile he had once fallen in love with, except that this was the false version. The one reserved only for him. "How nice," she continued. "You came to the door. I feel so honored."

Sol just looked at her through the designer shades, determined not to engage. "Hi, Katy," he said evenly. "Are the boys ready?"

Katy turned her back on him and called into the house. "Boys?!"

Then she turned back to Sol. "I heard about your last debate," she said, and the mock smile faded like an old photograph left out too long in the sun. "You caused quite a sensation."

Here we go, Sol thought. *Well, I'm not gonna play. I'm just gonna cut this one off at the knees.* "It's not much," he said, smiling his own counterfeit smile. "But it pays the bills."

Now, it was Katy's turn to grimace. "You know..." she start-ed, before letting it trail off. "Oh, what's the use? Forget it."

"No," said Sol, as if jumping bad with some knucklehead at a bar. "No, you want to say something, go ahead."

Katy turned back and flashed him a look combining conde-scension and exasperation. "Sol," she said, "I really don't need your permission to speak."

"Do we really need to do this? How 'bout I just pick up the boys and—"

"You know what? I want to talk about what kind of support you're giving our children."

Bingo! thought Sol. *Bing-what-you-wanna-call-your-freakin'-oh! She just punched the PIN code into that ol' ATM known as Sol Harkens. I do not need this!* This is why God created law-yers...If there were a God, which there isn't, then he would have created lawyers to soak the life out of him, monthly support payment by monthly support payment. Disso-mat Harkens.

"Oh," he sneered. "That's what this is about? Well, if you want to get the court to increase the payments, your lawyer knows where to find mine."

"I wasn't talking about financial support!" Katy exclaimed, closing the door behind her so the children wouldn't hear.

"What a novelty!" Sol exclaimed with as much sarcasm as he could muster. "Thank heaven for small blessings," he con-tinued, smiling when he said "heaven."

"What do you think it does to your sons," said Katy, "when they read about their father saying that their brother's life had no meaning? That there's no hope that he's in Heaven?"

"I don't believe in that fairy tale." Sol shrugged, like a kid denying that the broken window had anything to do with his baseball.

"Well, *they* do!"

"That's not my fault. I'm not the one who brainwashed them!"

"Don't you think it provides them with some comfort?"

"It provides them with an illusion."

"Assume you're right," said Katy, enunciating every syllable, "which, of course, you will. How can you rob them of that? You really believe they don't think about their brother every day and wonder if maybe they'll get the same cancer one of these days themselves?! It runs in families, and they know it! You think they don't lie in bed at night thinking about that? Hoping that their brother is in Heaven, pain-free?"

"They've never said anything like that to me."

"How could they, when your answer to everything is 'Party on!'? How can you take something so intensely private as the death of their brother and use it as part of your carnival act?!"

"Hey," said Sol, "that carnival act pays the alimony around here!"

"And who pays the emotional bills?"

<hr />

All right, thought Sol. *You wanna go there? Well, then, let's bring it on.* "You think there's a day or night or hour that goes by that I don't think about our son?"

"You know, my guess is that any time you do, you get so high there's not an actual feeling or thought at all."

"That's why they call it self-medication! Because it deadens the pain!"

"No, that's why they call it denial! Is that what you recommend for our children? Get so loaded you can't feel a thing?! That's the hope you want them to cling to?"

The problem with debating Katy was that she was actually better at it than he was. So he sulked instead of meeting her head-on.

"This conversation is not only pointless. It's painful."

"That's the first honest thing you've said."

"Then why don't we end it?"

Katy turned back toward him, crossing her arms. "You *did*! Remember?"

That was it. That was the button. She knew right where it was, and she pushed it every single time.

"You know why I ended it?!" He said loudly, no longer caring whether his kids could hear or not. "Because I got tired of living with you *constantly* praying for the salvation of my soul! I got tired of hearing your prayers to the God who, if you really believe in his omnipotence, killed our son, and if not killed him, sure didn't answer your pious entreaties to save him! Where were his love and his grace and compassion when you prayed for just enough of it to save an eight-year-old child who never did a thing except bring joy into the life of everyone who ever met him?!"

He hurt her with that, he knew it, and he was glad. Let her feel the pain that he did, that she masked with all her pious hosannas while she passed judgement on his vodka and Valium.

"You know what's so awful about your bitterness, Sol?" she said, no longer scoring points but with real sadness. "It's robbed you of the ability to remember the gift of that joy and left you with nothing but anger."

"Hey...Like I said. It pays the bills."

Just then, twelve-year-old Connor and fourteen-year-old Gus came banging out the door.

"Hi, Dad!" Connor said, hugging his father, with something of the little boy still left inside the pre-teen.

"Hey," said Gus, with nothing but fourteen-year-old cool.

Sol and Katy both sheathed their bloodied swords for the sake of the children, who knew they had just been cutting each other to ribbons.

"Uh, hi, guys," Sol said, awkwardly. Then, to Katy, "We won't be too long, Katy. I've got my book launch party tonight."

"I thought we were going to Bianco's Pizza Place and then going to spend the night at your house?" said Connor, disappointed.

"Pizza works for me, but I've got to work tonight, Buddy."

"Dad, is the launch party work?" Gus asked.

He looks just like his mother when he says that, Sol thought, so he gave him exactly the answer he would have given her.

"It pays the bills."

"Is there a party I could go to that would get me a raise in my allowance?" Connor asked.

"No," Sol said, with finality. "Not until you get an agent."

"I'll let you guys work this out," Katy said. "Sol, always a pleasure." She closed the door, and he heard her bare feet padding across the hardwood floor.

Sol and the boys started walking toward the Benz.

"So, is this another 'how to hate God' book?" Gus said.

Sol choked down the bile rising up. Gus even had his mother's inflections. "No, it's another 'how to think rationally' book."

Connor, unlike his brother, was still young enough to not care about religious debates. His tastes ran to pizza, video games, amusement parks, and his allowance. "Dad, you know, over at Bianco's, they have this really cool video game. I mean, it's old school, but it's so cool!"

Sol turned to Gus, hoping to find common ground in video games if nothing else.

"How about it, Buddy? Do pizza and video games interest you?"

"First, please don't call me 'Buddy,' Dad. I like my name."

He gets more like his mother every day.

Sol turned to Connor. "No more 'Buddy.' They grow up so fast!"

They got into the Benz and Sol gunned the engine, like a teenager trying to impress a rival, slammed it into reverse, and peeled rubber down the street, away from the home that once had held so much joy and from which, now, he could not wait to escape.

CHAPTER 4

The bile was still in Sol's throat. He felt the acid rising up and knew that the tomato sauce and pepperoni would only aggravate what he only somewhat sarcastically referred to as Divorced Bowel Syndrome.

On the other hand, Bianco's Pizza Place was a palace of nostalgia.

In a world of online gaming and fidget spinners, it was decidedly old school. It had bumper cars. Whac-A-Mole. Skee-Ball with actual prize tickets. It even had one of those little crane things that picked up the truly tackiest carnival prizes in the world, but which made you feel like a Nobel Prize winner, Olympic gold medalist, and undisputed heavyweight champion of the world if you ever succeeded in landing the carny "big fish."

And, miracle of miracles, they not only had vintage video games from a more innocent age, like Pac-Man and Asteroids, but they also had...pinball. And not just any pinball; they had old-school, rubber-bumper, two-fisted-flipper, light-flashing, bell-ringing, that deaf-dumb-and-blind-kid-sure-plays-a-mean-pinball, full-tilt, all-American, quarter-machine pinball.

Connor loved it. Gus could not have cared less.

"I love this place," Sol said.

"Me too!" said Connor.

They were finishing up a large pepperoni and black olive pizza. Hoping to find middle ground, Sol turned to his middle son and said, "Pizza's pretty good here, too."

"Nitrates," Gus said gloomily.

Sol felt the tomato sauce rising into the full acid-reflux region of his thorax.

"Can I go play the pinball machine, Dad? Please? I finished eating."

"Sure," said Sol, overjoyed to find a kindred spirit who happened to be a blood relation.

"Wait! I need some money!"

"Of course you do," Sol said, then thought, *what the heck*, and gave him a twenty. "There ya go, buddy."

"Wow! Thanks, Dad!" Having been successfully bribed by his father, an elated Connor ran off to pinball heaven.

Sol turned to Gus. "Is it okay if I still call *him* buddy?"

Gus's eyes instinctively rolled, the telltale sign of a teenager.

This is it, thought Sol, fishing a Tums roll out of his pocket and chewing four in one bite.

Then there was the silence, punctuated only by the sounds of amusement park games that his teenaged son no longer found amusing.

"So," Sol said, in the desperate silence created by Connor's absence. "How are things going with you?"

"Okay."

"School?"

"It's okay."

"Girls?"

"Dad!" Gus exclaimed disapprovingly.

"So much for stimulating conversation."

They were silent again, and then Gus sent out feelers, like an infantry company commander sending a squad out to probe the enemy's positions.

"We got a new youth group leader. His name's Nathan. He's really cool."

"Youth group at?"

"The church, Dad, duh."

"Of course." Sol sighed. "So, what's so special about this new guy, Nathan?"

"Nothing, I guess. I just like him. We're raising money to go to Haiti to help build a water system."

Sol just looked at his son quizzically. "A water system?"

"Uh huh."

"Is that a euphemism for a well?"

"Yeah!" Gus said, with unabashed pride. "And there's gonna be—"

"A hole in the ground. You want to go to Haiti to dig a hole in the ground."

"Look, if you're just going to make fun of it, then—"

"I'm not making fun," Sol interjected, laying the same trap into which so many Christian apologists had fallen and broken their dialectical necks. "I just wonder what the point is." He dropped his voice to a basso profundo. "Can't the people of Haiti dig? Do you have to go down there and show them how to do it? I'm willing to bet they've been digging holes in the ground for millennia."

"Why do you do that?" Gus asked, hurt tingeing his voice.

"What did I do?"

"Dad, I'm going to do this," he responded, leaving no room for doubt in his commitment. "I'm not asking you for money."

If there was one thing Sol knew without a doubt, it was that when Gus said, "I'm not asking you for money," it was going to cost him plenty, one way or the other.

"Well, trust me, pal, if you're getting the money from your mother, you're still getting it from me."

"I got a job, okay? At the yogurt place. And I'm *saving* the money!"

Sol looked at his son with newfound respect. "Oh, well, I'm sorry. I mean, I'm proud of you. That's...that's very impressive. And maybe you can treat me to a frozen yogurt one of these day too, so..." Sol tried to dig himself out of the hole into which he had just thrown what little relationship still existed between himself and his teenage son.

"I believe in God, Dad," Gus added, making his case. "And I know that's hard for you, but trust me, being the Christian son of the most famous atheist in the world...It's not exactly easy for me, either, you know?"

There was, without a doubt, a new maturity in the boy, which made Sol all the more protective. "Look, I just don't want you getting taken in by all this—"

"All this *what*, Dad?"

"It's a racket! You're going to Haiti. You think someone's not making money off the travel? You think they're not going to make an inspirational video about helping the poor, downtrodden Haitians dig a hole in the ground and use that for fundraisers? I know about marketing! It's what I do for a living!"

"I know," said Gus. "But it's not what our church does!"

"Give me a break," Sol replied dismissively.

"Dad, I'm going to do something good!" Gus looked his father straight in the eyes with a look so reminiscent of Katy. "Don't you even believe in doing good deeds?"

"Of course I do. I just don't believe in professional do-gooders."

"Dad, I'm not asking you to believe in the church. I'm asking you to believe in me."

Well, there wasn't anywhere Sol could go with that one. The kid had stopped him dead in his tracks. He felt the beginnings of genuine respect. "Fair enough. You're a very decent young man. And I'm proud of you."

"Thanks. That...means a lot to me."

There was silence, but it wasn't uncomfortable. There was heart and understanding in it.

"Gus, can I ask you something?"

He was about to ask Gus about his deceased older brother. He was about to ask about what Katy had said. He was about to ask if Gus and Connor ever worried that what had happened to their oldest sibling might happen to them as well. They had been so young, but they had experienced it all; if not exactly the sleepless nights, then the two overwhelmed and exhausted parents who lacked sleep, patience, and even tenderness sometimes. If not the vomiting itself, then the sound and smell wafting down the hallway, like a visit from the bogeyman. If not the loss of a child, then at least the resulting devastation and the annihilation of the family that had loved that child and brother.

So, Sol wondered, did they consider the chances of getting the same death sentence for themselves, what further destruction might ensue? And, finally, did they really think their brother might be in some kind of fantasy Heaven, happy, healed, and hopeful?

"Sure," said Gus.

"Your Mom said..." Sol immediately reconsidered. He was afraid of the answers to his profound questions, though to himself, he only admitted to preferring to stay in this rare moment of mutual respect in which father and son had, despite themselves, found some kind of a connection. And so, he took the coward's way out. "You know what? Nothing. I've had my quota of soul-searching conversations for the afternoon. You want to go play some video games? Asteroids?" he asked, knowing Gus's one weakness.

Gus looked at him evenly. "Sure."

"Bet you twenty bucks I top your highest score," Sol said, so looking forward to just playing with his kid.

But Gus sprang his own trap. "I'm not betting. I'm saving my money...to go help people dig a hole in the ground, remember?"

"Fine!" Sol said, in abject surrender. "I'll give you twenty bucks if you top my high score!"

Gus grinned from ear to ear. He had just bested his old man, and he knew it. "You're on!"

For the moment, they were father and son again. And life was no more complicated than pizza and video games. Of course, each of them knew that wasn't true. Each of them knew that life could end in tragedy at any moment, and the ghost of sadness hung, as it always did, between them. But, for the moment at least, death, if not vanquished, was being self-medicated with Asteroids and pinball.

CHAPTER 5

The Manhattan Museum of Art was all atwitter with the glitterati and literati of the Upper West Side, Sunday Book Review scene. These were the literary descendants of all the gang down at Elaine's. They were there to see and be seen at a launch party for Sol Harkens's latest tome, *Aborting God: The Reasoned Choice.*

There was a definite hierarchy amongst the guests, and certainly, some were more equal than others. There were the few remaining owners of private publishing houses, that rarest of all breeds, including the legendary Maurice Guibert, Sol Harkens's original publisher.

Guibert, at ninety-eight, was the very last of a renegade breed of avant-garde and, at times, pornographic publishers.

His father, Jack Muldane, was an Irish Protestant from Belfast who had married a French heiress by the name of Marie Guibert.

Born in 1919, Guibert lived a rather idyllic childhood in Giverny, whose bucolic landscape was forever immortalized by Monet. Muldane had been a contemporary of Ezra Pound and Sylvia Beach, who owned the Shakespeare & Company bookstore and whose claim to fame had been being one of the earliest publishers of both James Joyce and a young, budding American journalist by the name of Hemingway.

In the early twenties, Muldane established Monolith Press and by the mid-thirties, he was publishing the early works of Henry Miller. Not recognizing Miller's literary worth, Muldane became Miller's patron primarily because he thought of the latter's work as high-grade pornography.

Maurice had fame, responsibility, and notoriety thrust upon him at the tender age of twenty when his father died shortly before the German occupation, making Maurice the youngest publisher of note, not only in Paris but in all of Europe. His literary legend grew during the time of the occupation, when he adopted his mother's maiden name to prove his Francophone credentials and play down his Anglican roots.

He was viewed by the Nazis as one of the purveyors of degenerate art, and thus, was forced underground, becoming a mixture of Resistance hero and swindling scoundrel. He purloined Nikos Kazantzakis's book, *Toda Raba*, and published it without the author's permission in a French edition shortly after Kazantzakis had returned from the Saint Catherine's monastery on the top of Mount Sinai in the Sinai Desert of Egypt. The monastery, in addition to being famous for its location, had a certain degree of infamy as the preferred place of exile for Greek Orthodox monks, whose questionable predilections landed them, ironically, atop the mountain reputed to be the spot where Moses received the Ten Commandments.

There were few facets of Guibert's life that more endeared him to Sol Harkens than the aforementioned association, by six degrees of separation, with perverse Greek Orthodox monks and the Mosaic origin of the Judeo-Christian ethic.

Having run afoul of the law in postwar France, Guibert headed for greener pastures in the urban jungle hideouts of Manhattan, where he published Beckett, Miller, J.P. Donleavy,

Marcus van Heller, and Vladimir Nabokov, becoming a literary legend in his own right during the Andy Warhol era and lasting as an icon all the way into the mid-nineties and the Clinton era, when it was rumored that he swapped cigar stories with the disgraced former president.

It was during that time that he signed an agreement to publish an obscure graduate student's work on atheism entitled *The God Myth,* for which he was said to have paid Sol Harkens the princely advance sum of five thousand dollars.

Part of Guibert's legend and lore was the fact that he frequently welshed on if not outright stole from, many of his authors, including the most famous amongst them.

Sol Harkens would prove not to be an exception.

After having paid young Harkens one thousand of the promised five-thousand-dollar advance, Guibert stiffed the neophyte writer for the remaining four grand. Sol, not to be trifled with, pushed his way into Guibert's surprisingly low-rent literary offices, festooned with framed first-edition book covers on the walls, and demanded his money. Guibert, as was his wont, demurred with a Gallic variation of "The check is in the mail."

Happily for Sol, he was wearing a two-button leather sports coat, which was all the rage amongst grad students at the time and afforded him enough protection to jab his elbow through the glass pane of Guibert's office window. He glanced about the office. "Let's see," he told Maurice, "what could you possibly have that's worth four thousand dollars?" Whereupon he spied a top-of-the-line Dell 486 with a cathode-ray tube monitor, which Guibert had only recently purchased to replace his trusty IBM Selectric.

"Ah!" said the young Harkens. "That looks like about four thou worth of technology to me!" And, so saying, with a semi-Herculean effort, he yanked computer, monitor, and keyboard from their hallowed spot on Guibert's desk and held them outside Guibert's now-broken window, twenty stories up from the sidewalk down below, demanding his money in return for not dropping the computer to its demise.

"Assassin!" Guibert hissed. "You are a madman!"

"I'm also getting to be a tired man," said Sol. "And my guess is, this computer's not going to stop on the sidewalk. It's going to stop on some passerby, and then you'll be sued. Because I won't be here."

"Not even Miller was this incorrigible! I lived through the Nazi occupation! At least Donleavy had the civility to sue me when I stiffed him! But you are like a Corsican thug!"

"Arms are gettin' shaky," Sol said.

"*Bien! D'accord!* I will write you a check," said the Frenchman.

"Maurice," Sol said, "that's actually insulting. Open your wallet, give me all your cash, and you'll get your computer back."

"*Incroyable!*"

"Hands are gettin' sweaty," Sol chirped, almost merrily.

"Fine! *Voilá!* Take your blood money!" Guibert produced two hundred sixty-three dollars from his wallet, and Sol dutifully pulled the computer back over the precipice and dumped it onto Guibert's desk. He then went to Maurice's file cabinet, pulled out his contract, tore it to shreds, and flung it, confetti-like, through the open window.

The rest, as they say, was history.

The God Myth became a hit.

Guibert sued him for breach of contract.

Sol countersued.

And four years later, they smilingly settled out of court when Guibert forked over close to half a million dollars for the paperback rights.

Sol maintained a soft spot in his heart for the ancient scoundrel, who immediately spotted not Sol but Vanessa Biechevskayo, the beautiful twenty-eight-year-old Russian supermodel du jour.

"Ah," cooed Guibert, in his charming Gallic accent. "Who is this enchanting creature?"

Vanessa possessed not only a willowy, statuesque Slavic physique but also the requisite pouty lips and almost feline eyes. "I am Vanessa Biechevskayo. I am with Sol."

"*Obayatel'nyy*," Maurice intoned, with a very passable Muscovite accent.

"Spasibo," Vanessa said. "Vy ponimaete Russkji?"

"*Ja ponimaju, nemnogo*," Maurice said, smiling his best Chevalier grin. "*Ne ochen' horosho.*"

"No, but you speak beautiful!" said Vanessa.

"My cousin on my mother's side was Anna Pavlova. She had an orphanage in Paris, at Saint-Cloud. My mother and the Comtesse de Guerne ran it for her. She was many times in our home and taught me the little Russian I know."

"Pavlova!" said Vanessa, impressed.

"There is not a word that he just said that is true," Sol said.

"I'm shocked!" said Maurice, staring at Vanessa's décolletage. "I gave the boy his start, and that is the gratitude? He denies my family's heritage? *C'est la vie.*" He kissed Vanessa's extended hand. "*Enchanté, mademoiselle.*"

"*Le plaisir c'est moi*," Vanessa replied.

"I'm gonna puke," said Sol. "It's America. Speak English!"

"Once a provincial," said Maurice, "always a provincial."

Just then, Sol heard the somehow lazy LA accent of his agent, Norm.

"Hey, pal! How you doin'? You killed the other night, okay? In that debate? You killed it! Maurice! You're still alive! How ya doin'?"

Norm was Sol's literary agent and as much a legend in his own right as Maurice Guibert. He had started out in the mailroom at MCA in 1948, turning down a tryout with the Brooklyn Dodgers to do it, and had been made an agent at twenty-one by no less than Lew Wasserman himself and was later mentored by the great "Swifty" Lazar. Before becoming a literary agent, he was known as what was referred to in the trade as a talent agent. At one time or another, there was no one he didn't represent. His first trip to New York was as the twenty-one-year-old agent of Jack Benny and George Burns. Later, he represented Fred Astaire *and* Gene Kelly, not to mention Sinatra and Elizabeth Taylor. In fact, he had been Taylor's agent when she had stolen Eddie Fisher from Debbie Reynolds and the two young lovers had hidden from the paparazzi in the posh dining room of MCA's Beverly Hills headquarters, where Liz endeared herself to one and all by making caviar omelets in the kitchen and serving them while singing *Tammy's in love.*

It was only after the Justice Department broke up the talent agency that Normie, as he was known to one and all, went over to the "dark side" and began representing writers. But despite almost five decades of representing literary folk, Normie still sounded like the Hollywood agent he had once been.

"I'm tellin' ya, he killed!" he said.

Tracee Houston, Sol's publicist, was there as well. Quick-witted and vivacious, with the most winning smile one had ever seen, she was a distant cousin of Whitney Houston and possessed almost as much star power. "This last debate is the one that will put the book totally over the top!"

"Thanks, Tracee," said Sol. "Wasn't a very high bar, as they say, but I cleared it."

"Killed. Trust me," said Norm.

Tracee smiled her megawatt smile. "You are a total rock star, boo!"

"An aging one, I'm afraid," said Sol, with feigned modesty.

"Hey," Norm said, "Mick Jagger could be your father."

"And who is this?" Tracee said, turning her gaze on the supermodel.

Sol gestured an introduction. "Oh, this is..." and he momentarily blanked on her name. He had already had two glasses of Champagne and three vodka martinis, so perhaps he couldn't be blamed. Russians, however, have a saying about people who can't hold their liquor, and Vanessa was not amused.

Cold as Stoli on ice, she said, "I am Vanessa Biechevskayo. I am with Sol. But only for party, unfortunately. I have sport magazine bikini photo shoot in Bahamas tomorrow. From here I go straight to airport and—"

"Fascinating," Tracee said, never one to share the spotlight with any other woman. "Well, you should leave early. Make sure you don't miss that flight. Airports are so awful these days."

"Killers," said Normie. "I can give you a lift, if you like."

Tracee turned to Sol, all business now. "I may have a hit for you to do tomorrow with Diane Sawyer; something with the whole 'ISIS is no different than the church' thing. It's gone viral, baby!"

"When's it air?" Sol asked, then realized, "No, wait! I'll be in the Hamptons. Will she travel? Or do a phoner?"

"Diane Sawyer? You're kidding, right?"

There was a hot, young band out of Brooklyn hired for the occasion, The Goods, playing a song called Cecelia Says, whose rhythms seemed to grab one, no matter how hard they tried to resist, and Vanessa was not in a resisting mood. She swayed to the song, gave Tracee a dismissive glance and Norm an enticing smile, then turned to Harkens and said, "Sol, darlink, I'm going to mangle."

"I think you mean 'mingle.'"

"Da, sure. Mingle, mangle, *yanye panyomayo*. Whatever. Is good I do it for business. No?"

"Absolutely," said Sol to Vanessa, who had already turned and swayed to the other side of the room to "mangle" with a few paparazzi. Sol turned to Tracee and said, referring to Vanessa, "Loves me like a rock."

"I'd say congratulations on the new relationship," Tracee began, "but I've seen the women in your life. How about the Diane Sawyer piece?"

"Sorry, babe. But I need some breathing space."

Just then, a waitress walked by with a tray of exotic-looking drinks and a form-fitting skirt.

"And what are these, my dear?" Sol asked, referring to the colorful beverages on the tray.

"They're called Harkens's Hedonists," said the waitress. "Our mixologist created it especially for the occasion. It's mezcal, with chili-yuzu-blood-orange sour and Drambuie, served 'up' in a frothy, frosty glass with burnt chili salt on the rim."

"Well, I can't say no to one of those! It'd be like denying one of my own children!" He took two glasses from the tray and offered one to Tracee.

"Not for me, thanks," Tracee said. "I'm driving."

"Well, in that case," said Sol, "I'll double-fist it and toast myself. Here's to me!" He clinked both glasses, draining one and then the other.

"Sol," said Tracee. "Diane Sawyer?"

"Tracee, this last week's been murder. I'm running on fumes. I'll be back next week. Just a short long weekend in the countryside."

"With Vanushka?" Norm asked.

"Vanessa," responded Sol.

"Hey," Normie said, grabbing a Harkens Hedonist for himself. "You say 'mingle', I say 'mangle'. Ya know what I mean."

Tracee adopted a hand-on-the-hip attitude. "Does she even read English?"

"Absolutely," Sol assured her. "I saw her with the Tiffany catalogue the other day."

Just then, Tracee's cell phone pinged. She checked her texts and said, "They're ready for you. Sylvie's about to introduce you."

Sol grabbed another Harkens's Hedonist and made his way into the lobby of the Manhattan Museum of Art, where a raised podium had been erected for the occasion.

Sylvie, Sol's chic but tough-as-nails publisher, motioned for him with a snap of her fingers, as if disciplining a pampered Pomeranian. "Have you forgotten why we're here?" she demanded.

"For the free drinks?" Sol replied, trying not to slur.

"Pull yourself together," she reprimanded him. "This is business!"

She mounted the podium and flashed her best Manhattanite smile, rising to her full five foot four inches, aided by her six-inch Jimmy Choos.

"Hello, everyone! I'm Sylvie Carlyle, and I have the great good fortune to be Sol Harkens's publisher." She paused to let that impressive fact sink in. "The first time I opened a Solomon Harkens book, it changed my life. Then he showed us just how clever he was when he signed with me!"

Assorted forced chuckles chortled their way through the room.

"His next book, we shepherded all the way to the top for twenty-three weeks!"

There was a smattering of applause, mainly from her underlings.

"He is sense in a senseless world, intelligence for the thoughtless, candor for the demented, and truth is his currency. So, I'd like to introduce a man of towering intellect, a fabulous writer, a great humanitarian, and one of my dearest friends, the bestselling author of the soon-to-be released *Aborting God: The Reasoned Choice*, the one and only, Doctor Solomon Harkens!"

Now there was genuine applause. Sol drained the last of his Harkens's Hedonist and bounded up to the podium.

"First, thank you all for coming tonight," he said. "My new book, *Aborting God: The Reasoned Choice*, is an esoteric look at the fallacies promoted by all the so-called 'True Believers'. From born-agains to jihadis, those who have abandoned reason in favor of religion are responsible for more misery than the plague of the Middle Ages."

He noticed that the more he drank, the more he sounded like the late Bill Buckley, and he couldn't help but admire the effect.

"And to those miiiiiiindless rednecks," he said, enunciating a distinctly Buckleyan pronunciation, "clinging to their guns and Bibles," he intoned, quoting a former and, in this crowd, much-missed president, "I make no apology for that comparison.

"My truth," he said, mustering all his alcoholic integrity, "is nonnegotiable, so there are no apologies. Religion," he said, fighting down an inebriated belch that would have made the late Foster Brooks proud, "has no business deciding for me what is right or wrong for my life, and that is why I've banished it, why I have, in my life, indeed aborted the very notion of God!"

Some society matrons in the crowd very nearly swooned. Even three sheets to the wind, his eloquence was undeniable.

"So, if you believe in the triumph of human reason over superstition and mythology, buy my book. Buy *two* copies, one for yourself and another for a misguided friend, if you hang around with that sort. God help us, pardon the pun, they seem to be in the ascendancy these days."

With the sound of applause ringing in his ears, Sol sought out and pried Vanessa away from the paparazzi and squired her toward his Benz as The Goods sang the last lyrics of "Cecilia Says," "This love of mine...you wouldn't know what to do with it..."

Paparazzi lightning flashes lit up their way as Sol tried to walk as soberly as possible. The attendant opened the door for him, while another opened the door for Vanessa. But she kept walking, instead, toward a waiting limo.

"Hey!" said Sol, crossing over to her. "What are you doing?"

"Sol," she said. "You are very handsome and very smart, and you are also very drunk. If you were Russian, it wouldn't matter. But you are not, so I have ordered limo."

"Hey, blow the photo shoot off and come with me to the Hamptons! I've got a great house rented. We could have a killer time."

"Yes, of course. But first, I must to do bikini shoot. Is big broke for me."

"I think you mean break."

"Da. Sure. But first, I do the photo shoot. Then I am back, and we can mangle."

She slid into the limo and blew him an air kiss.

"Don't I even get a kiss goodbye?"

"Sol, darlink, there are paparazzi and I don't want to ruin the makeup. You understand. Is business."

"Not personal," said Sol, sulking.

She flashed her model smile. "See how smart you are?!" Then she blew another air kiss to Sol and a final one to the paparazzi.

Her limo pulled out in one direction.

Sol got into his Benz and pulled out on the opposite side of the street. As he did, he saw Maurice Guibert getting into his own limo with the young waitress in the form-fitting skirt who had earlier been handing out Harkens's Hedonists.

Maurice smiled at Sol and raised his cane in mock salute, leaving Sol with nothing other than a bottle of vodka perched between his legs for comfort.

CHAPTER 6

Sol fishtailed out in a U onto 53rd in what he hoped would be a bad-boy salute to the Russian supermodel who had just blown him off because she had the audacity to doubt his abilities as a driver with a blood-alcohol level that was barely three times the legal limit, not including the diazepam he had popped just before the launch party to still the waters of what was, evidently, a case of the pre-show jitters. He also hoped that his senile, cane-waving, cradle-robbing former French publisher, Maurice Guibert, would take note of the smell of burning rubber spewing from his Mercedes-Benz CLS 550 Coupe.

Fifty-third street, he determined, was a fine venue for driving when slightly inebriated and recently stood up by a Russian supermodel. He ruminated on the face and form of Vanessa Biechevskayo. He had to hand it to that one, despite the fact that she had blown him off for a bikini shoot in the Bahamas. She was certainly no wuss, though he believed the Russian expression was a bit rougher around the edge, and certainly more descriptive.

Though born in Leningrad, her father, a passionate devotee of Gorbachev and *glasnost*, had been arrested by an obscure young major in the First Directorate of the KGB by the name of Vladimir Putin. The latter's duties consisted mainly of monitoring foreign diplomats, but he became so enraged at the sight of Anatoliy Ivanovich Biechevskayo protesting the anti-Gorbachev forces in the regime that he personally arrested the elder Biechevskayo and had him charged under Article 58-11 as an enemy of the workers, a traitor, and a saboteur, the punishment for which was eternal internal exile in Siberia.

Thus, Anatoliy Ivanovich Biechevskayo, his wife Lushinka, and their newborn infant Valeska (which Vanessa would later change to a more anglicized and easily pronounceable appellation) were transported courtesy of Soviet-era boxcar to the northeasternmost hinterlands of Siberia, the very definition of isolation; a town inaccessible by road, buried under ice and snow eight months of the year, and dipping below temperatures of -60 Fahrenheit, known as Chersky. It was there that Anatoliy Ivanovich, once an associate professor of Russian literature, became an embittered alcoholic and remarkably resourceful hunter. The last thing that was needed in the frozen tundra above the Arctic Circle was a professor of anything, especially literature. Happily, Anatoliy's grandfather had been a hunter, as had his father before him, and he had trained his young grandson in the archaic and almost lost arts of animal tracking, hunting, skinning, taxidermy, and smoking in order to preserve the meat for as long as possible. The now undeniably beautiful Vanessa Biechevskayo had grown up on a diet of arctic wolf, the occasional bear, and not a few rodents. Indeed, she possessed, to Sol's mind, almost wolfen teeth, exceptionally pointed canines that revealed themselves on the rare occasions when she allowed her pouted lips to smile anything other than the prepared grin and tossed hair reserved for paparazzi.

And this Russki had blown *him* off because he'd had a couple of drinks?! He was offering her a long weekend in the *Hamptons!* A chance to rub elbows with the most elite of the East Coast illuminati! And instead, she opted for the Bahamas and some long-haired, tatted-out, cigarette-smoking, limey Brit photographer, all so she could land a couple pages in the bikini edition of a sports magazine?! He was Sol Harkens, man! When Clinton was going through his worst adversities, it was a toss-up as to whether he was gonna call Tony Robbins or Sol. *So, big deal,* Sol thought. *I can't do the fire dance. But I know Bill! I call him "Bill," not "Mr. President"! He always says, "Call me 'Bill,'" so I do! And he calls me "Sol"! Sol and Bill, Bill and Sol! We hang together! We've golfed together! I let him cheat!* Sol thought drunkenly, but then immediately discarded the thought because everybody let him cheat. He was, after all, the former president. *Bahamas,* Sol thought. *Sand fleas.*

Sol gunned the CLS 550 through Lexington Avenue, immediately discarding the notion of heading uptown to 60th and dropping in at Le Veau d'Or. It was a weeknight, and Kathy would probably be closing the joint by now, anyway.

No, prudence suggested that he continue down 53rd, past the Citigroup Center, and head toward Fifth Avenue. He could hang a right on Madison, head back up to 60th, hang another left on Fifth, and head straight for his favorite watering hole, Harry Cipriani, right next to the Sherry-Netherland Hotel. He would bypass the usual bellinis and head straight into martini land, straight up, shaken, not stirred, with a twist.

Thus, he neared the site of the former Stork Club at 53rd, just off Fifth. *I was born too late*, Sol ruminated. *The Stork Club and I would have done just fine. That's when people knew how to live! They all smoked, drank martinis, and wore tuxedoes.*

*Speaking of martinis…*he remembered the bottle of vodka in his lap, grabbed it by the neck, and took a swig. Just then, the hands-free phone rang.

Hands-free is one of the greatest inventions ever made, he thought. *They oughtta give the guy who invented it the Nobel Prize. It leaves you one hand to steer and the other one to drink!* Sol pressed the little telephone button on his steering wheel and drunkenly slurred, "Yeah," into the speaker.

"Hey, pal," he heard Norm's laid-back LA accent intone. "That Vanushka made you look great!"

"Odd," said Sol. "I thought it was the other way around."

"Trust me. Nothing like a six-foot-tall Russki supermodel to enhance the old image."

Sol took another swig of the vodka. "I'll drink to that," he said, raising his bottle in salute.

"By the way," added Norm, "does the commie have a sister? An aunt? A well-preserved grandmother, maybe? Any port in a storm, know what I mean?"

Sol smiled at Norm's egalitarian attitude toward the gentler sex. "'Fraid not. She's one of a kind, more or less."

It had begun to rain. Not a heavy rain, mind you, just enough to loosen the oil on the scum-soaked streets of Manhattan, bringing them to their slickest, most dangerous levels.

Sol flipped on the wipers, with their reassuring, Germanic-precision swish-and-thud. It then occurred to him that he had driven past Cipriani, and was back at 53rd. So he hung a quick left on 52nd. "Well, at least I've got one glamorous model that I know how to handle."

"What are you talking about?" Norm asked.

"This Benz. CLS 550. Takes the curves like it's on railroad tracks." So saying, Sol took another swig of the vodka, hung a left onto Madison, jammed back onto 53rd, and then, totally discombobulated, took *another* series of lefts onto Fifth, then 52nd, then onto Madison, and back onto 53rd.

He realized he was going around in circles. That's when he saw the parked garbage truck, which seemed to be rushing toward him, though, in fact, it was the other way around.

He slammed on the brakes.

The tires slipped against the newly liberated oil of the rain-slicked street, and the Benz began to hydroplane.

"Well, drive safe there, pal," Norm spoke, oblivious to the approaching disaster. "And honestly, check out what the Russki's grandmother looks like. Not that I'm desperate, but I'm not picky, either."

Sol's Benz swerved to the right, hopped the curb, and slid on the wet grass straight into Paley Park, which, oddly enough, was on the site of the former Stork Club. Sol's foot slipped off the brake pedal and back down onto the gas, causing the ever-responsive Mercedes-Benz CLS 550 to leap like a young gazelle at the roar of a lion, straight into a tree.

Norm heard the sounds of the crash through his cell phone. "Sol? SOL?! Are you okay?! Sol, you drunken idiot, don't you die on me! We got a book tour!"

But Sol, for his part, could no longer hear Norm. Nor was he any longer in the Mercedes CLS. He seemed to be in a tunnel of sorts, on the curves of which were projected scenes that looked oddly familiar, until Sol realized two things. First, he was no longer drunk. In fact, he had never felt such clarity in his entire life. And second, the scenes projected on the tunnel in which he now found himself were of his own childhood.

Puppies.

Mommy.

Beach sand castles.

His seventh-grade school locker.

His first ten-speed bike.

And as he hurtled through the tunnel, he was also aware of the fact that he was rising up out of the wreck of his Mercedes-Benz CLS 550 Coupe and rushing into the nighttime sky, up and up, until the earth was but a speck, a white circle in a black background that vanished as he jumped to light speed through the tunnel that now seemed to be made of light itself. Yet, despite the speed, it was peaceful. He was surrounded by the sounds of light breathing, or perhaps it was music, and light all around that, somehow, he thought he could hear, which, in turn, was odd, he thought, because light was something one saw. And yet, this light had to it physical properties. It was sound. It was warmth. It was beyond warmth. It was, Sol realized to his amazement, what he could only comprehend as...love.

And there, at the end of that tunnel, bathed in what the world's most famous atheist truly thought of as heavenly light, he saw his beautiful, healthy, radiant eight-year-old son, his pretty boy, his poor child, his Davey.

The little boy reached out his child's limbs to his father and hugged him to his sweet self, called him "Daddy," kissed his cheek, and tightened his arms around him as Sol wept as he had never wept before.

"Davey!" he cried. "My son! My son! Davey! My son! My son! My son!"

He held his child to him, tighter than a drowning man clings to an outstretched hand about to pull him from the deep.

"I love you so much!" he said, and felt bathed in a sense of joy he never dreamed existed.

He smelled the sweet smell of Davey's hair, that scent he remembered so well, felt the softness of his child's skin, and then heard a voice say, "It's not your time, Sol. You have to go back."

"What?" said Sol with an anguish as great as the joy he had just known.

"It's not your time, Daddy," his child explained, with timeless wisdom.

Sol felt himself begin to be pulled away, away from his son, away from his boy, away from his sweet Davey. "No! I don't want to leave! I want to stay with you!"

"Daddy." His son smiled the most beatific smile. "Let there be light!"

"What?"

Davey smiled a smile that was pure love. Indeed, Sol felt bathed in that love, as Davey said again, "Let there be light, Daddy!"

And a heartbroken Sol Harkens felt himself pulled back and down, past stars and puppies, bicycles, the smells of his mother's cooking, past the Manhattan skyline, as he screamed, "NO! I DON'T WANT TO LEAVE! I WANT TO STAY WITH YOU!!!" and awoke in the ER trauma room of New York Presbyterian Hospital as Doctor Shell supervised the placement of defibrillator paddles on his chest and yelled "CLEAR!"

Sol felt his body jerked back to life with the electric current, opened his eyes, tried to focus on the doctor and nurses in their scrubs, and screamed with the anguish of a soul suddenly lost forever.

"NO! I'M BACK!"

CHAPTER 7

B oth the local and national New York paparazzi were packed as tightly as sharks around a newfound bleeding carcass at the entrance to New York Presbyterian Hospital. The reporters for the city editions of *The New York Times*; *The Wall Street Journal*; *The Daily News*; *Newsday*—which was technically not part of the New York media, because of its publishing headquarters in Millville—the *Post*, which few people realized and if they had, even fewer would have cared was founded by Alexander Hamilton in 1801; *El Diario la Prensa*, New York's largest, and the nation's oldest, Spanish-language daily publication; the predominantly African American *New Amsterdam News*; *The Village Voice*; *The Jewish Voice*; the NYC-based correspondents for ABC, FOX, NBC, and CBS, as well as their cable affiliates, MSNBC, Fox News, CNN, and HLN; FBN; the always-aggressive TMZ; the completely irrelevant MTV; the local public broadcasting affiliate, WNET; WNYC Radio; NY1; WCBS; as well as the online outlets of Huffington Post and Buzzfeed; the East coast editions of the *Hollywood Reporter* and *Variety*; *The Blaze*; *The Christian Science Monitor*; and, because of the importance of the possible death of the world's leading atheist, The 700 Club and CBN.

All jostled for position, hoping for a glimpse of a grieving family member, preferably a teary-eyed widow, until some of the paparazzi condescendingly reminded what they laughingly referred to as their colleagues that Sol Harkens was divorced, and his ex-wife, being a Christian, would not likely be teary-eyed, either because she hated his guts or because she took comfort in the idea that he might have had a last-minute conversion and was on his way to being reunited with his Lord and Savior, Jesus Christ, though few but the reporters for CBN would even entertain such a possibility.

Together, the tribe of paparazzi representing either the cream of the crop of New York media or the scum of the pond thereof, depending upon one's point of view, elbowed, shoved, drove Jimmy Choo stiletto heels into the toes of competitors, and surged forward and then back again like the ebb and flow of a surging tide as they met with the resistance of the hospital's security staff augmented by New York's Finest, most of whom had not a clue as to who Sol Harkens was, much less the importance of his demise or miraculous escape from the jaws of death.

There was no statement forthcoming from the hospital. There had simply been a transmission someone had picked up on a scanner, referring to the fact that a barely living Sol Harkens, last seen at the Manhattan Museum of Art for the launch of his latest book, *Aborting God: The Reasoned Choice*, had been transported from Paley Park, site of the bygone glories of the Stork Club, to New York Presbyterian.

Just then, an SUV of the type usually reserved for diplomats or media personalities who thought of limousines as being too un-proletarian and decidedly ostentatious, pushed its way through the shark-infested waters of paparazzi, and disgorged Sol's agent, Normie Zee, and publicist, Tracee Houston.

The police and hospital security guards pushed the yipping and yapping paparazzi aside like Chuck Heston parting the waters of the Red Sea, in order to allow Sol's hired-gun mouthpieces to gain entry into the hospital.

Questions were shouted out as desperately as pleas for help from drowning passengers of the *Titanic* for any tidbit of news that might be tossed their way.

"Is Sol Harkens dead, Normie?!" one TMZ reporter shouted out.

"Am I wearing black?" Norm replied.

"No," came the reply.

"Then, until I am, he's not!" said the legendary Norman Zee. "None of my clients are dead until I say they are."

Not to be outdone, Tracee Houston pivoted on her Manolo Blahniks, to make sure the TMZ reporter got her en face, and shouted, "He's doing Diane Sawyer! How could he be dead?"

The two pushed their way past the flotsam and jetsam of what passed for journalism in America and made their way past the line of security and into the hospital.

Inside Sol's private VIP suite, Doctor Shell—who, Sol secretly suspected, had changed his name to some Anglicized version meant to hide his obvious South Asian ancestry—read from the iPad that had replaced what Sol thought were the far-more-romantic metal file holders he associated with every doctor's bedside scene he could remember. Whether it was Alan Alda or whoever that jerk was that they called Dr. McDreamy, or the Robert Young portrayal of Marcus Welby, MD, or Vince Edwards's immortal Ben Casey, or even Tim Conway's comedy sketches with Harvey Korman, they always had metal file folders. They hung on the bed, they made a satisfying clang when swung shut, and not a one of them had ever crashed. There was something about these doctor iPad things that Sol mistrusted intensely. What if his had been hacked? What if the doctor had simply keyed in the wrong one?

Sol Harkens had certainly responded inappropriately to wrong emails or text messages. He had sent declarations of love to his accountant, and bank statements, regrettably, to inamorata both past and present, including the Russki whom he thought of as being responsible for his near-fatal accident.

That thought, triggered by the iPad, flashed in a second as random thoughts tumbled through his mind, until suddenly, he remembered Davey's angelic face, the sweet smell of his boy, his tiny arms around his neck, the beatific smile as he said, "Daddy. Let there be light," and the horrific sense of loss as he felt his soul, a word he normally loathed, being pulled away from that of his son. And he remembered the anguished cry with which he had awakened, and that triggered in him the memory of the cry that had poured out of him at the news that his child, his sweet Davey, was dead.

It had felt as if he had been hit in the gut by George Fore-man in his prime. He remembered his body flying backwards as if literally struck by the news, the wind being knocked out of him as his back hit the wall. And the horrible cry of "NO! NNNOOOOOOOOO!!!" which no amount of drugs or al-cohol could ever blot out, which came back to him nightly, woke him from his dreams screaming, or took hold of him, still awake, as the narcotic numbness eased just enough to let the anguish back in.

It was the most horrible sound he had ever heard in his life, and it was his, forever, an audible mark of Cain, a curse that never left him.

"Aside from the concussion," Doctor Shell droned on, "you have a serious blood clot that, if it breaks loose and travels to your brain, will cause a stroke."

"I had a stroke?" Sol asked, not really caring, just wanting to know what still worked and what didn't. Because the truth was, life held neither interest nor attraction. He wanted to be back with Davey. That thing he had thought of as death before was now the only form of life for which he longed.

"You're not listening to me," he heard Doctor Shell say with a kind of jovial bedside manner. "The stroke was the bad news. The good news is there is a very good chance that, if you're careful—you are already on massive amounts of blood thinners—with proper supervision, you can make a full recovery."

"I'm not going to die," Sol muttered, unable to disguise his own sadness at that realization.

"Not if you follow doctor's orders."

"Well, there's a comfort," Sol said, the irony not lost on him. But he had no desire to share with this little medical clerk what he could only think of as the miracle he had just experienced. And so he smiled and said, "Thanks, doctor. Whatever it takes, I'll do it."

"It takes rest, first and foremost. Complete rest. You know, it's a miracle...clinically dead in the ambulance for four minutes."

"Four minutes," Sol repeated, amazed, himself, that he had been out that long, and no less amazed at all he had experienced in less time than it takes an Olympian to run a mile.

"Evidently," said Doctor Shell, "it just wasn't your time."

"Of course it wasn't his time!" Sol heard Norm's 'Hail, fellow, well met' delivery. "He's got a book tour! I'll tell him when it's his time!"

"You jerk!" Tracee interjected, whacking Normie's arm and putting her hand on Sol's knee, then removing it just as quickly as she turned to Shell. "Is it okay if I touch him?"

"Everything but his head," Doctor Shell intoned, with not a little severity. "He has a nasty concussion and a blood clot, but I should think he will survive your hand on his knee."

Tracee replaced her hand on Sol's leg. "How you doin', boo?"

"Headache," Sol replied.

Not one to leave a word dangling, Norm completed a thought that everyone had either ignored or forgotten. "I'm kidding! He knows I'm kidding, right, pal?"

"Could you keep the decibel level down, Normie? The head really hurts."

"I said, I'm kidding," he added softly. "You know I'm kidding, right, pal?"

"About my death?" Sol asked, blearily.

"Well, sure," replied Norm. "What else would I be kidding about?"

"Right," said Sol. "Absolutely. I know you're kidding. You wouldn't be able to commission my funeral."

"Who's talking commission? I'd stream it live!" Norm bellowed, enchanted at his own wit. And then, remembering Sol's pain, he reduced his volume to a stage whisper and repeated, "Who's talking commission? I'd stream it live!"

Sol's head was spinning.

"Well, I'll just leave you folks alone. It really was a miracle," Shell added as he left the room.

Sol felt he had to tell someone or he would burst. He looked at his manager and his publicist and let the words tumble from his mouth. "I think I saw my son."

Tracee leaned in conspiratorially. "I saw Katy pulling in behind the hospital. She'll probably be here soon, but I didn't know she brought Connor and Gus."

Sol shook his head slightly. "No, I saw Davey. I saw my boy."

Both Tracee and Norm were silent.

Norm looked at Tracee. Tracee looked at Norm. It was as if both of them were thinking that their ship had just hit an iceberg and within moments, they would discover, to their horror, that there weren't enough lifeboats to go around.

Norm turned to Sol. "Try that one again. In English."

Sol reached out his hand and took Norm's. The latter was surprised at how warm Sol's hand was.

Sol was equally surprised at how cold and fishlike his agent's hand felt to him. "I'm not kidding, Norm. I saw Davey. I was in this tunnel of light and—"

Norm took Sol's hand in both of His, in that way agents have of trying to express solidarity and friendship. "Really?" he said. "Fascinating!" He smiled what agents thought of as smiles and what really resembled nothing so much as an obligatory grimace. "Keep that one to yourself, whaddaya say, pal?"

Sol looked quizzically at his agent. Keep it to himself? He wanted to shout it from the rooftops. He looked to Tracee for some sign of encouragement, but instead, she sat on the edge of his bed in a sign of intimacy, and said, as if confiding some secret that ought best to be left untouched in the attic, "You had a very bad concussion, Sol. It's only natural that you would have hallucinated."

Sol tried to sit up, but the pain in his head throbbed so badly, he rested back against the pillow. "It wasn't a hallucination. It was as real as both of you are."

"Actually, I'm not that real," said Norm. "I'm an agent. Remember?"

Sol withdrew his hand from Norm's clammy grip. "I know what I felt, and I know what I saw."

Norm got the same expression on his face that Don Corleone got when instructing Luca Brasi to find out what Sollozzo was really up to. Nothing personal, strictly business. "Of course you do. But don't broadcast it, pal. Pretend you saw Sasquatch, Elvis, Freddy Krueger. Catch my drift?"

"I saw my son, Norm! And I felt...the most perfect love I've ever experienced in my life."

"I had a night like that once," Norm said. "In Vegas. And I didn't have to flip a Mercedes-Benz for it, either."

Sol turned away from his agent. He felt his eyes beginning to well up with tears of emotion, and there was no way he was going to share it with Norm.

"You saw what you wanted to see, Sol," Tracee said in a soothing voice, taking Sol's hand. "And it's perfectly understandable." She leaned into Sol's line of sight, forcing him to look into her eyes. "But it wasn't real."

There was a long silence in the room, a palpable one. A deal wasn't being offered; it was being dictated. What Sol saw wasn't real, that was the deal. Those were the words, and there would be consequences if they weren't followed.

Sol's publicist and agent let that sink in for a minute.

This wasn't a game, and near-death experience or no near-death experience, this was business. Sol was their racehorse, and they intended to ride him, not see him retired and put out to pasture without even the occasional stud service payment.

The silence spoke volumes, and then Norm broke it with that forced agent joviality. "Besides, I've booked you the comeback lecture!"

Tracee joined in. "This is it, Sol, bottom of the ninth, fourth quarter, and you've gotta sink a three-pointer."

"I've never heard anyone so totally mangle three completely different sports in one simple sentence," Sol said.

"Whatever," Norm said. "You catch the drift. Just be who you've always been, and this is the payday."

"What payday?"

Norm looked at him as though he were a dimwitted child. "Don't you get it? You've come back from the dead! Just like that other guy, what's his name?"

"Lazarus?" Tracee asked, remembering her early Baptist upbringing.

"No," quipped Norm, "Arsenio Hall."

There was no joke in Norm's last remark. There was nothing in Norm's life that didn't have a show business reference. He had no idea who Lazarus was; it sounded like a punk rock group more than a person.

Once again, the silence invaded the room. The awkward kind, when no one has an idea of what to say, when nothing seems appropriate, as if someone has made an off-color remark and everyone else is too embarrassed to speak, a kind of verbal breaking of the wind.

These were the kinds of moments that Tracee truly hated. Silence was an enemy. It was a void she felt compelled to fill. "I tell you, I nearly had a heart attack myself when they told me you had died!"

"Who said I had died?" Sol asked.

"Sol, honey," Tracee replied, the down-home accent coming back. "Everybody thinks you died."

"And that's what's going to make your comeback an even bigger story!"

"Norm," Sol said, trying to explain, "I've just had the most profound experience of my life. I don't care about a comeback. I don't care about the book tour. Do you get that?"

"Absolutely!" Norm answered, trying to fake sincerity as best he could. "Sol, you get a conk on the head, you see things! I understand that. Tracee understands that. The *doc* understands that! We all do!" He leaned in. "Plus, the doc said the old blood alcohol level was—"

Just then, Sol heard the familiar voice of his ex-wife. The intonation was what he remembered, even more than the sound of her voice. It was the accusation.

"You were *drunk*?!" Katy asked incredulously as she entered the room and closed the door behind her.

In a way, Sol was grateful for her presence. Her tone of voice snapped him back to a reality with which he was far more comfortable...sarcasm.

"Katy," he said, smiling the smile he reserved for his ex-wife. "What a pleasant surprise. How did you—"

"I guess I'm still on the notify list," Katy said.

Despite himself, Sol couldn't help but notice what an attractive woman she still was. More than attractive, she was beautiful.

If only she wasn't such a...Christian.

Tracee tried, once again, to fill in the gap. "Hi, sweetheart! Thank God our boy is okay, huh?"

Katy was having none of it. She kept staring at Sol with that look in her eye. "Sol, you were drunk? Is that how this happened?"

Norm moved up to take a defensive position, like a goalie trying to guard a sure-thing penalty shot. He had to nip this one in the bud, and he knew it. "He wasn't drunk," Norm answered on Sol's behalf. "He had a drink. One. At the launch party." And then he couldn't help but add, "Like any normal person."

"A normal person?" Katy said. "As opposed to a Christian?"

"Your words, not mine," Norm answered. "I have nothing but the greatest respect for—"

"Oh, please," Katy interrupted, dismissing him with a wave of her hand.

Norm knew that wave of Katy's hand meant trouble, and so he went into full damage-control mode. He could spin faster than the teacups in Disneyland on the best day they ever had. "There was no police report. Nothing. It was a rainy night, car lost control. As a matter of fact, we're considering suing the manufacturer."

"We've already released a statement," Tracee continued, falling into the party line.

"And that's the one we're sticking to, no matter what," Norm concluded.

Katy looked from Norm to Tracee, then to Sol. "I'm not talking about damage control," she said to the two flacks. She pushed between them and leaned in toward her former husband. "I'm talking about a minimum of self-control! Sol, you've got two boys who love and need you. Two boys who've already lost a brother. How could you..."

The pain in Sol's head was excruciating now. Under the best of circumstances, Katy had that effect on him, but these were far from the best of circumstances.

"Katy, I don't know if blood pressure can make the blood clot I've got break loose and kill me, but how 'bout you ease off the sermon until my pain meds kick in. Okay? Then, knock yourself out."

"You have a blood clot?!" Katy asked in horror. "You have a blood clot, and it can break loose and kill you?! Is that what you're saying?!"

"I'm saying there's certainly less of a chance of it, Katy, if you would just—"

Norm stepped between them. "Let's not squabble, kids. Let's talk about something more pleasant. For instance, money! I've got feelers out to all the prime cablers and digital platforms. A one-hour talk show." He said, looking at Sol. "Huh? Huh? Huh?"

"He's right," Tracee added. "Sol, you're gonna be the next Bill Maher."

"And you know why that is?" Norm asked.

"I'm taller than he is?"

"Everyone's taller than he is," Tracee chuckled.

Now it was Norm's turn to lean in toward Sol. He put his hands on Sol's hospital bed and whispered what he assumed were the magic words. "You're the only one who can say, 'I crossed over to the other side and there's no *there* there. The only *there* is *here.*'"

The hospital lobby was packed with reporters and paparazzi who had pushed their way past security. An orderly paid off by the *National Enquirer* had just confirmed that Sol Harkens was not only alive and well, but about to be discharged.

To save time, Doctor Shell brought the discharge papers up to Sol's room while Tracee went down to see how big the crowd was. She was not looking for a way around them; she was looking for the best way to take advantage of them.

She was, after all, a publicist. By the time she got back up to the hospital's VIP suite, Sol had finished signing all the forms for his release. The doctor asked to take a selfie. Sol obliged.

Then the doctor gave him a referral for a follow-up visit, wished them all well, expressed his admiration for Sol's latest book, and left them all to their own devices.

Tracee said, "So, there is just an eensie-weensie, teensie little group of reporters outside. What're we gonna say if they ask if you had a near-death experience?"

"We?" asked Sol.

"What near-death experience?" Katy asked.

"It's just a figure of speech," Norm said.

"Tracee, Norm," Sol said. "I'll be fine. Okay?"

By now, he had been transferred into a wheelchair, in which, by hospital policy, he was to be discharged.

Out of instinct, he handed his plastic hospital bag to Katy. "Here. Could you carry this for me?"

"Really, Sol?! Really?!" Katy said, remembering all the undisguised, genuine hurt at being nothing more than an appendage to the great Sol Harkens. "I think I'm through carrying your baggage." She was a tall, statuesque, beautiful woman. And when she bent down toward Sol, her physical presence still had an effect on him. "I'm glad you're not hurt. I thank God for that," she said, stressing the word "God" like a divorced wife twisting the stiletto. "And like it or not," she continued, "I'll be praying for you." She said it genuinely enough, but it still sounded like a threat to Sol. Now, however, she was all business. She was a mama bear, defending her children more than concerned about her former mate. "But you need to get help, Sol. Not just for your sake, but for your children's. They love you and they need their father, and they don't need any more tragedy in their lives."

She let that line hang there in the air between them.

War between divorced couples is never pretty, and it's never Marquis of Queensbury rules. It's head butts and rabbit punches. It's dirty. And each one knows exactly where the other one hurts the most.

"Do you get that, Sol? They've had enough tragedy. So if you think you can drink yourself to death or drive when you're drunk and kill yourself and maybe some poor, innocent people, then it's time to man up and live, if not for your sake, then your children's. 'Party on' isn't going to solve this; it's what caused it," she concluded, as only an ex-wife could hurl an epithet.

"*Almost* caused it, Katy, darling!" Norm said. "But thank God, to use your phrase, our boy is still with us! And 'almost' only counts in horseshoes...and hand grenades. We're going to have to get off on the next floor, babe, so maybe—"

Katy turned to Norm. She had never liked him before, but she despised him now.

"Maybe I shouldn't be there?" she said, actively challenging him to say the words.

"Sweetheart." Tracee tried to smooth the waters. "I think the focus ought to be on the good news that Sol is okay."

There was the silence again.

The business deal on the table.

The unspoken reminder that Sol's atheism, and the books it spawned, paid the alimony and the child support.

But Katy wasn't having any part of it.

"Hey," she said, "the show must go on, right? You know, Sol, one of the perks of no longer being on this merry-go-round is that I no longer have to take being 'handled,' or talked to like a child. I retired from the circus a long time ago."

"Hey," said Norm cheerily. "*No problemo.*"

The elevator doors opened. Katy pushed a button to take her up to another floor. "I'll just get off at the parking level."

She stepped back against the wall.

"It's showtime, folks!" Norm said. "Here we go!"

He pushed Harkens's wheelchair out of the elevator and into the lobby full of waiting press.

CHAPTER 8

Flashbulbs, like monsoon summer lightning in the Rockies, exploded in Sol's brain as Norm pushed the wheelchair into the waiting school of piranhas.

Anyone who thinks atheism isn't a religion, and an orthodox one at that, has only to examine how they react to the apostasy of one of their own. They don't eat their young; they devour them, rip flesh from bones, and fight over the bloody guts.

And that is in neutral territory.

New York, Los Angeles, and San Francisco, it might be said, are to atheism what the Vatican, Mecca, and Jerusalem are to what are sometimes referred to as the big three, television networks and car manufacturers excluded.

Microphones and cameras shoved in toward Sol's face, and, quite literally, the spittle of salivating reporters rained down upon him.

"Dr. Harkens! Did you die in the car accident?" mouthed a hair-gelled television reporter.

"Were you clinically dead?" asked a scruffy one who was clearly from the print media.

"Did you see the other side?" inquired another representative of what is referred to in the trade as "the hairspray talent."

"Do you believe in God or logic?" That particular query came from a reporter who was obviously vertically challenged, as his head appeared only occasionally as he jumped up and down behind the first row of members of the fourth estate.

"What message do you have for your fans?" a WNET reporter and Kent-Brockman-lookalike shouted. For some reason, the letter "F" in him produced a veritable flood of phlegm.

Sol wiped his face and felt a wave of nausea engulf him. This was not the erudite Dr. Harkens to whom one and all had become accustomed, the rapier wit, the Muhammad Ali of debaters. He knew that he looked confused, unsure of himself, even afraid, and suddenly, he felt very old.

"I, uh...I'm not sure about the dead part."

He looked, desperately, for a friendly face in the crowd, some ray of encouragement, but he saw only alley cats clawing for a piece of the carcass that he now felt he embodied.

"I think the death thing may have been somewhat exaggerated."

He was trying desperately for the Mark Twain quote and missed it like a three-point shooter on a cold night. The attempted witticism bounced off the rim, and he didn't even have a shot at the rebound.

"What about the tunnel of light?" the *Post* reporter yelled above the din. And again, on the "T" sound, Sol felt the *schpritz* of New York journalism.

What is it with consonants and these guys? he thought.

"Did the near-death experience change any of your views or strengthen them?"

The guy who asked the question held a microphone with a sock over it that must have been dripping wet. He had a lisp on the "S" sound that would've made a Castilian monarch proud.

Actually, Sol thought, *he sounds more like Sylvester the cat than Juan Carlos the king.*

He expected the man to say, "Thufferin' thuccotash!" at any moment, and, indeed, it would have made just as much sense as anything else the reporters were saying. And that, for some reason, triggered a loop of Mel Blanc doing Tweety Bird inside his skull.

"I tought I taw a puddy tat! I tought I taw a puddy tat! I did, I did taw a puddy tat!"

It got to a point that Sol wondered what would happen if he actually said it. Would they quote him?

The drugs, whatever they had given him, he had to admit, were awfully good.

And so, he decided, what the hey? He'd give it a try.

"I, uh..." Sol said, and the room fell quiet, awaiting his pronouncement; the first words from one who had peeked behind the veil of this mortal coil and come back to describe what he had seen.

"I, eh..." said Sol thoughtfully, as if trying to find the words that could accurately portray that which lies behind the heavenly membrane marking the boundaries between what we call life and death.

They leaned in toward him, mouths suddenly silent, microphones outstretched like hands in supplication to a saint or, more than that, to Moses, just come down from the mount.

"I, uh," Sol repeated, milking it for all it was worth, "I tought I taw a puddy tat!"

The reporters looked from one to another, and they looked back at Sol in what could only be described as shock and awe.

An NY1 reporter leaned in, even more closely. "You, you what, Doctor Harkens?"

Sol was about to lay the "I tought I taw a puddy tat" line on him once again and then amplify it with an "I did! I did taw a puddy tat!" when Norm shattered the spell.

"Give the guy a break, huh?" interrupted the legendary Normie Zee.

"What did he say about a 'puddy tat?" asked a mustachioed reporter, who Sol suddenly realized was Geraldo Rivera. "Did he actually say he saw a 'puddy tat?'" Geraldo demanded.

"Let me draw a map for you," Normie Zee said, staring Geraldo in the eyes. "He didn't say he saw a 'puddy tat.'"

Rivera wanted to push the issue, but could see that Normie Zee was zeroing in on Capone's tomb as his next retort, so he backed off.

"He *definitely* said *something* about a 'puddy tat'!" CNN's Brian Courier insisted.

"Doctor Harkens has had a severe concussion," said Normie Zee, enunciating every syllable. "He did not see God. He did not see the abyss. He did not see a tunnel of light. And he did not. See. 'A puddy tat.' Are we all clear on that?"

Again, the room fell silent.

"I heard him say 'puddy tat,'" MSNBC's Donna Flanagan muttered under her breath. It was clear she was mulling as to whether or not to go with that. The story was "puddy tat."

Could she sell it? There were so many avenues it opened up. Harkens was putting them on! Harkens was having a break-down! Harkens was a stroke victim!

Wait, that one was the kiss of death. If she was making fun of someone who wanted to say "pussy cat" but couldn't and said "puddy tat" instead, even if he'd actually *seen* the afore-mentioned pussy cat, she'd have the entire stroke community up in arms against her. It was a dealbreaker. Reluctantly, she let the 'puddy tat' angle slide.

"Doctor Harkens," yelled Norm above the electric din of cameras, mics, and lights, "has, as I've previously said, suffered a severe concussion, and he will give a complete account of that, and all of his injuries, at his upcoming lecture."

Tracee Houston flashed her publicist's smile, adding, "Which will be at the Jewel Box Theatre next Tuesday, 8:00 P.M. Eastern on TNN, and streamed live at www.AbortingGod.com."

The security guard, who had most certainly heard Doctor Harkens declaim that he had, indeed, tought he taw a puddy tat, decided that he'd had enough, too. He pushed himself into the crowd and, in the thickest of all possible Brooklyn accents, hollered, "All right, get outta here. Alla y'uz don't have to go home, but y'uz can't stay here. Go on! Get outta here!"

Sol leaned back and let the morphine kick in. He looked at the security guard and in the softest possible whisper said, "But, I did. I did taw a puddy tat." Then, he thought of his child, and the memory unexpectedly made him sob uncontrollably, his body heaving with every sob.

<hr />

Back in Sol's uber-hip West Village, loft, Tracee and Norm walked a very stoned and mildly limping Sol Harkens into his abode.

The loft was his sanctuary.

It sat atop one of the few period buildings that boasted both a doorman and a 1930s elevator, the kind with a fold-down velvet seat for the elevator operator and the ship-like, engine order telegraph control that encompassed a full half-circle in either direction in order to move the elevator up or down.

The loft itself was a sanctuary and respite from the ravenous city streets down below, and each wall contained a different homage to some facet of Sol's career.

There were the movie-poster-sized blow-ups of book covers.

There were Andy Warhol-esque quadrants of Harkens's psychedelically colored likenesses.

There were shelves containing various plaques and literary awards, two Peabodies, and one Emmy for his PBS series, *The God Myth*.

There was even a separate shelf for an Oscar awarded to Sol Harkens for Best Documentary. It was a 1993 effort that had become to atheists what *An Inconvenient Truth* would become to climate change fans and what *Roger & Me* was to those who viewed various American auto makers as capitalist pig oppressors of the masses; polluters of the planet; mass-murdering poisoners of defenseless, brown-skinned children; and, in general, the objects of all the hatred generated at a G20 summit in Hamburg, Germany.

The film that had earned the aforementioned Oscar was entitled *The Argument for Darwinism: Case Closed*. It was viewed as the ultimate theatrical defense for the theory of evolution, one that allowed absolutely no possibility of divine intervention. Humanity was as much a random accident as the supposed works of Shakespeare were produced by a hundred unbelievably dedicated and hardworking monkeys, typing nonstop on a hundred typewriters, for an undetermined portion of eternity, during that time the simian auteurs would produce the complete output of the immortal Bard.

The fact that every writer in the English language, and all their collected works over a period of four hundred years, had produced absolutely nothing even remotely close to rivaling— let alone eclipsing—Shakespeare put not a dent in the theory of the hundred literary monkeys, of which Sol Harkens had become the staunchest of defenders.

Mind you, he was not a defender of the theory, but of the hundred monkeys assiduously typing away at the hundred mythical typewriters, that could somehow produce the works of Shakespeare. *That*, he thought to himself, *was nothing more than a huddled mass of intellectual shenanigans, folderol, and ballyhoo.*

No, Harkens', concern was not the theory, but the imaginary typing pool of dung-hurling, literary chimps. Did they get lunch breaks? Were they unionized? Were there lumbar supports in their chairs? Did they suffer from carpal tunnel syndrome, which they could then report to OSHA in order to receive just compensation? Were they doomed, like galley slaves, to type forever, only to be dismissed by a *Simpsons*-esque Mr. Burns figure for one spelling error? No, Harkens was all for the monkeys.

It was the Shakespeare part that pushed his literary buttons.

Indeed, the very subject of Shakespeare was enough to set Sol Harkens off.

If, indeed, there was anything in Sol Harkens's universe that was a bigger myth than that of the existence of an omniscient, all-powerful, benevolent deity, it was that the semi-literate grain merchant and third-rate actor known as William Shakespeare could *possibly* have written the plays that bore his moniker.

"Consider," Sol said to Norm and Tracee, "that whoever wrote the works of Shakespeare had, beyond the slightest shadow of a doubt, *had*, mind you, to have extensively traveled in Italy! And it is equally known, beyond a shadow of a doubt, that Shakespeare, the immortal beard—not Bard!—had never left England! Do you know that the statue commemorating Shakespeare in Stratford-upon-Avon portrays him carrying a sack of grain because that's what he was known for? He was a freaking *grain merchant!* And later generations were so embarrassed by the fact that the only monument to the supposed greatest writer in the history of the English language in his hometown had him holding a sack of seed! And you know what they did? To try and make him seem even just the tiniest bit literary? They affixed *tassels* to the *corners* of the aforementioned *grain sack!* The immortal Bard! That the author of *Hamlet*, *Romeo & Juliet*, *Julius Caesar*, the creator of such indelible characters as Puck, Lady Macbeth, Iago, the artfully camouflaged Polonius, Prince Hal, and the Wellesian Falstaff could be, as a tribute to his literary prowess, could be portrayed as a man holding, for no apparent—or remotely fathomable—reason a tasseled pillow as a tribute to his artistry is, I must say, more absurd than *anything* the worst Christian apologist has ever come up with! Do you know that Shakespeare, at his death, possessed two books? Arguably the most prolific literary mind in the history of Western civilization, a man with an intimate knowledge of the workings of royalty, Italian usury, the Machiavellian maneuverings of the Danish court, the author of that most inspiring of military speeches, which commemorates St. Crispian's Day as that which will forever be remembered by that happy few band of brothers, *that* William Shakespeare possessed a library consisting, mind you, *in toto*, of two freaking books?! Puuuuuhleeeeeeaaaase! The author of the sonnets, the greatest love poems in the English language, written, in all likelihood to a fourteen-year-old boy, left to his wife, Anne Hathaway, the supposed object of his ardor and affection, not even his Lilliputian library of two books, but, all in all, he bequeathed to this supposed inamorata his 'second-best bed'?! That's what Anne Hathaway, wife of Shakespeare, got from this supposed most passionate of all lovers, the author of the balcony speech and the immortal words of Cleopatra's main squeeze, *that* Anne Hathaway, got from the supposed author of the works of William Shakespeare? His second-best bed?! She didn't even get the tasseled sack of grain?! And these bumpkins, my supposed literary kindred spirits in debunking the myth of Jesus, actually subscribe to this literary fairy tale? The story of Jesus, by comparison, even I admit, is Aristotelian logic compared to a belief that the works of Shakespeare were actually written by the original Slick Willy! It makes me want to puke!" Sol exclaimed, and then thought, *Lord in Heaven*, not without a small degree of self-irony, since he was, after all, the world's foremost atheist, *Lord in Heaven above, THESE are some great drugs!*

He then proceeded to projectile-vomit onto his antique, refurbished, three-hundred-year-old hardwood floor.

"I'm not cleaning that up," moaned Normie Zee.

"Do you need anything?" Tracee asked, after the caregiver they had called cleaned up that which the drug-induced, Shakespeare-debunking Sol Harkens had spewed across his loft.

"Nah, I'm good," Sol replied, feeling like a stranger in his own apartment. "I just want to rest."

"If you need anything at all, you just say the word."

When Tracee said it, there was no doubt in Sol's mind that she meant every word.

"Because," added Norm, "we're family, right?"

And of course, when Norm intoned his undying fidelity, Sol had no doubt that he meant not a word of it.

"Absolutely," said Sol.

Tracee kissed Sol's cheek and put his hospital bag down next to his leather sofa, which faced out onto the loft across the street.

"Now," said Norm, "we've got a great future, as long as we stick to the game plan."

Sol nodded, and Norm mischievously added, "And no more puddy tats."

"Banished forever," Sol said.

Norm gave him a manly hug, and then patted Sol's back, thought better of it, and pulled away. "Sorry about that. That didn't hurt, did it?"

"Not at all," Sol lied.

"All right, then," Tracee said, before she and Norm beat what Sol decidedly felt was a hasty retreat.

There was more that Sol had wanted to say about Shakespeare, but his audience had departed.

He looked around his empty loft, dropped his keys by the door, and limped over to the bar. He poured a tumbler full of vodka with which to wash down his pain pills, ensconced himself on his vintage leather couch, and reached for one of the four remotes, for each of which he reserved a special loathing. None of them ever seemed to work.

He pushed "On" for the cable box, "On" for the TV, and "On" for the sound system, and all he got was a blue screen. Then he remembered to unplug the HDMI cable hooked to the Roku box, and cursed softly as the screen stayed blue, flashing the words "NO SIGNAL. NO SIGNAL. NO SIGNAL."

He popped two OxyContin, a couple hydrocodone, and a diazepam chaser, and washed it down with some of Potocki's finest.

Okay, he thought, *the cable's on. The sound is on. The monitor's on. There's a blue screen, and it says "No Signal." Why can't they just do on and off? That worked. It worked all through the fifties, the sixties, the seventies...okay. Let's turn them all off, then we'll turn them all on again. Let's start with the sound.*

He pressed the sound remote, and the strains of Pavarotti singing the aria "Nessun Dorma" wafted out from his surround-sound speakers.

"Ah!" he exclaimed. "Problem solved!"

He switched the sound from DVD/CD to VIDEO, then turned on the cable box and then the monitor and *voilà*! Simple as pie, there was the smiling visage of Mario Morales, he of the sculpted abs and gleaming teeth, the new host who had replaced the previously disgraced host of *Dateline Hollywood* who had been unceremoniously booted for his secretly recorded conversation concerning the sexual musings of the most loathed presidential candidate in recent history. And since there was nothing the media could do to the candidate, they took their righteous indignation out on the unfortunate former host who, all in all, had said nothing different than what any of them had mouthed on thousands of occasions. His only crime was being caught, and the only reason he was caught was to out the sexist, misogynist, racist, homo- and islamophobic, thuggish pig who somehow, despite every poll, in which modern-day journalists place their faith as much as ancient Romans trusted haruspic priests—who predicted the future by examining the entrails of sacrificial sheep and poultry—had managed by an as-yet-unfathomable conspiracy to illegitimately seize the presidency from their candidate of choice.

Hence, Billy got the boot, and Mario of the flashing, Zorro-esque smile got the coveted catbird seat on the Hollywood gossip show du jour.

And these people believed Shakespeare actually wrote a single word of the works ascribed to him!

Sol leaned back into the sweet and familiar comfort of his antique leather couch and settled in for a little Hollywood gossip, only to hear Mario say, with a decidedly snarky delivery, "And on the lighter side, Russian beauty Vanessa Biechevskayo, after the near-death experience of her former main squeeze, Dr. Sol Harkens, seems to have found true love in the arms of the very-much-alive photographer Brad Steele while they were on a photo shoot in the Bahamas."

And there before the now-besotted Sol was the telephoto-lensed photograph of the tatted-out, stringy-haired, six pack-abbed, twenty-nine-year-old, limey photographer romping with Sol's bikini-clad, Russian former lady love in the Bahamian surf, as the Brit heartthrob made an obscene gesture to the snooping paparazzo with the telephoto lens, while Vanessa, realizing they were being photographed, did her familiar head-toss, parted her pouted lips, and flashed her wolfen grin as the two walked arm in arm into the tropical sunset.

Sol, salving, if not a broken, then at least a somewhat chipped heart, popped another OxyContin, raised his tumbler of vodka in mock salute, washed down the pill, and said to no one in particular, "Here's to my lady love."

He then, somehow, managed to find *Shakespeare in Love* on the Classic Movie Channel and saw Gwyneth Paltrow give a passable recitation of the grain merchant's "What's in a name" speech, before vomiting once again.

The rest of the night was, oddly, a blur.

CHAPTER 9

It was a fitful night, with the phrase "Double, double, toil and trouble, fire burn and cauldron bubble..." repeating again and again in his ear. He awakened to the ubiquitous sound, known to every New Yorker, of the garbage truck beneath his window at some ungodly, predawn hour.

The television was still on. Shakespeare had long since ceased to be in love and had been replaced by a carnival barker hawking a miracle cloth that could, as a proven scientific fact, soak up three hundred times its weight in liquid. This, considering the amount Sol had vomited, he decided, was not only useful but completely indispensable.

He stumbled to the television monitor and managed to scrawl the 1–800 number onto the palm of his hand. He called the number and a man with a decidedly South Asian accent introduced himself as Johnny and asked how he could be of help.

"Wipe-Wowies," Sol managed to croak.

"Yes?" asked the Pakistani Johnny.

"I want 'em."

Johnny began to read from his script of special offers; buy one-get two free, or was it buy two, get one free? It didn't matter, because Sol wanted six cases.

"Six cases?" Johnny asked. "Oh, my! It will take me some time to figure out the discount. So many Wipe-Wowies!"

"I got time," Sol said. "That creeps in this petty pace, from day to day, to the last syllable of recorded time."

"What's that, sir?" Johnny asked.

"Come, wind! Blow! Wrack! At least we'll die with harness on our back!"

"I beg your pardon?" said Johnny.

"Just mulling," said Sol. "You believe in Shakespeare?"

"Do I believe in—"

"Shakespeare," Sol demanded. "Do you believe that Shakespeare wrote the works of Shakespeare?"

"Why would they be called the works of Shakespeare if Shakespeare had not written the works of Shakespeare?"

"Do you believe in God?"

"Oh, most definitely," Johnny said. "And I also believe you are entitled to a sizeable discount. And if you place your order with me today for the six cases, I can also give you two Miracle Mops for the price of one."

"What's so miraculous about the mops?"

"Well, to begin with, you can take the head off and put it in the washing machine. It is made of nine thousand continuous strands of thread, woven together."

"Nine thousand?!"

"Continuous strands, woven together."

"That's miraculous!"

"Exactly! Which is why they call it a Miracle Mop. Which is probably why they call the works of William Shakespeare the works of William Shakespeare."

"I don't get the connection, but I'll buy a dozen of those, too."

During the next twenty minutes, Sol Harkens became the proud owner of six cases of Wipe-Wowies and one dozen Miracle Mops. Moreover, he paid an additional thirty-six dollars to ensure a next-day delivery.

The transaction having been concluded, Sol popped an additional three diazepam, a healthy slug of vodka straight from the bottle, and Mumbled, "Is this a dagger that I see before me? Come, let me clutch thee…wait! 'tis a Wipe-Wowie! But, what's in a name? Would not a Wipe Wowie by any other name smell as sweet?"

So saying, Sol Harkens fell into a deep and peaceful slumber, only to be aroused, he thought, some five minutes later by a constant buzzing.

He slapped at his face to kill the obvious mosquito.

It wouldn't die.

It buzzed again.

He slapped again.

In seeming mockery, the obviously immortal mosquito continued to buzz.

He slapped a final time, and still, the mosquito miraculously escaped.

Two things now dawned on Sol Harkens.

The first was that he had a splitting headache from having repeatedly slapped himself in the face.

The second thing was that the buzzing sound, which he had mistakenly attributed to an insect, emanated instead from the buzzer located on the right-hand side of his door.

"Sol!" He heard Tracee's irritatingly cheerful voice. "It's Tracee! Let me in!"

She buzzed again, then knocked.

He pulled himself up off the sofa where he had fallen asleep, tripped over the bottle of vodka sitting next to it, spilling its contents onto his antique hardwood floors, and tripped his way toward the door.

"I'm coming! What's your problem?"

Sol opened the door, revealing his publicist holding a bag of takeout Danishes and two lattes.

"The doorman just let me come up, hope you don't mind. I didn't think you'd be entertaining."

"How'd you know I wasn't up here with Vanessa?"

She pulled a latte out of its cardboard holder and handed it to Sol. He sniffed at it, made a face, and put it down on the counter. She put the Danishes in the microwave and pushed REHEAT.

"Well, first of all, they said on TV that—"

"I know. Brad Steele."

"Well, he *is* really sexy."

"And he's twenty years younger. And has six-pack abs. Wait a second, there's an open wound around here somewhere on my body. Make yourself at home and pour some salt into it. Some vinegar. Or maybe a bit of lemon juice."

"You're such a tease." The timer on the microwave went off. Tracee opened the door, pulled the Danishes out, saw nothing but dirty dishes in the sink and in the dishwasher, and so tore off a paper towel, put the Danish on it, and handed it to Sol. "Watch out, it's hot."

Sol took a bite of the Danish. The icing seemed to burn his tongue and melt the roof of his mouth like carbolic acid. He spit the Danish into the sink and reached for the coffee, which was boiling hot so that now the roof, tongue, and sides of his mouth felt like they had third-degree burns.

He spit the coffee into the sink.

"I told you it was hot! Anyway, Sylvie called and she wants me to draft your talking points for the lecture tomorrow night. I told her I felt I had to clear it with you first."

"Good," said Sol. "How about, 'no.'"

The vodka bottle that had been standing by the couch was now on its side, and empty. So he went to the bar and opened a new one.

"We both thought you might react that way."

"You were both right. Now, if you'll excuse me, I'm a little down on my allotted vodka consumption for the day. Also, it's *not* hot." He scooped a handful of ice from the freezer into a glass that still contained the remains of last night's consumption, poured in a stiff shot, and took a long sip.

"Sol, this would just be an aid for you. Like a teleprompter. In fact, we'd like you to have a teleprompter. Just in case, you know?"

Tracee picked up the fallen, empty vodka bottle and took it to the recycling beneath the kitchen sink. It was overflowing with similar bottles. "Loooooooooocy? You got some 'splainin' to do."

"I've been adhering to a strict liquid diet. What of it?"

Tracee crossed over to Sol and looked him straight in his bloodshot eyes. Her tone was now dead serious. Not a bit of friendship. All business. "This is the audition gig for the cable talk show, not just another speech. Can you honestly tell me you're a hundred percent on top of your game?"

"Absolutely," Sol belched. "One hundred fifty proof. I mean percent."

The Jewel Box Theatre was exactly what its name implied. It was on 44th between 7th and 8th, and was a little gem of a theater, a nine-hundred-seat house with gilded boxes and ornate chandeliers.

Sol had stopped first at Angelo's Pizza, right next to the Ed Sullivan Theater, and gotten a small pepperoni with black olives and a glass of passable Sangiovese. If you liked New York pizza, Angelo's was the place. They still had coal-fired ovens that dated back to the 1800s and gave the crust a satisfying, blackish ash and the taste of a hundred years of pizzas backed into it.

It wasn't Italian pizza. It wasn't thin-crust Margherita pizza. You could get the best of those across from Carnegie Hall at Trattoria Dell'Arte, where Sol invariably started at the Nose Bar for an ice-cold vodka martini and deep-fried artichokes, *carciofi alla Giudìa*. They were bite-sized artichokes you could pop into your mouth one whole one at a time, deep fried and salty. They were the best Italian appetizer in the world. You could get them at Cafe Fiorello's across from Lincoln Center too. The same guys owned both places. And the pizzas were authentic Italian with thin crusts.

But they weren't New York pizzas.

There was nothing thin-crust about New York pizzas.

They were thick and man-sized, meant to hold a worker over till end of shift and made to be eaten with the kind of wine they used to derisively call "Dago Red." Good, cheap Italian wine with a bite to it that could stand up to the hearty taste of a real New York pizza.

Sol finished off a bottle of the Sangiovese and then walked down from 56th to 44th. He turned right to the Jewel Box. There was an alleyway just before the theater where he turned right again and hung a left, past the garbage smells, to the stage door of the Jewel Box.

The black stage attendant, whose name was Ross, greeted him. "How you doin' tonight, Doc?"

"Above ground and out of jail," Harkens replied. "All the rest is gravy."

"Ain't that the truth?" Ross admitted Harkens into the darkened, backstage world of the Jewel Box Theatre.

As glamorous as the place was out front, with its gilt-edged railings and velvet seats, that's how big a rat trap it was backstage.

Most New York theaters were like that.

The dressing rooms never had any of the glamour you saw in Fred Astaire and Ginger Rogers movies. They were tiny and smelled of mold. The plaster was usually cracked or falling off the walls or ceiling. Water pipes gurgled and hissed, and toilets were so noisy, they could rarely be flushed during a show lest the audience think an earthquake was in progress.

They used to smell of cigarette smoke, but that had long since been banned in New York. On the other hand, there was no legislation against open bottles of alcohol, and the smell of many an actor easing the pre-show jitters was a ubiquitous one.

Sol made his way to the dressing room they had reserved, where a thermos of coffee had been pointedly placed.

There was a knock at the door, and the stage manager, whose name—like all stage managers'—was Max, said, "Half hour, doc."

There was a makeup table and mirror, and Sol considered the fact that he did, indeed, look like death warmed over. He didn't particularly care.

He would have loved a drink, but none was to be had.

On the other hand, he mused, that's why God created Valium.

He reached into his pocket, pulled out the vial, and popped two with a sip of the brackish coffee from the thermos in front of him. He was having a case of the pre-show jitters.

Well, perhaps "jitters" wasn't the word. Tremors was more like it.

"Come on, baby," he said to the Valium, "kick in!"

He hated being cooped up in the dressing room and so made his way through the rabbit warren of subterranean hallways built for actors who had lived a hundred years before and were evidently much thinner.

He took the metal, spiral stairway up to stage level to see Tracee waiting for him. "Are you ready?" Tracee asked.

"This isn't my first rodeo, kiddo." He stepped to the edge of the wings, where he could see Sylvie, who, because of her diminutive height, was perched on a box behind the podium from which he would speak.

Sylvie, his publisher, in her late fifties, was still hot. She had that sparkling kind of brown eyes, the right kind of porcelain-pale New York complexion, and for a short girl, a dynamite set of legs. She glanced over into the wings and breathed a sigh of relief upon seeing Sol. Sol gave her a smile and a wave, and she continued her introduction. He peeked through the curtain at the edge of the wings and saw that they had a full house. That only increased the jitters, so he popped another Valium.

"And so," Sylvie said, "it is my great honor to present the person who helped me shed superstition and find reason, a man of towering intellect, a great humanitarian, a fabulous writer, and one of my closest personal friends, Doctor Sol Harkens!"

The applause reverberated off the walls. There was nothing like coming close to death to encourage the fan base.

Sylvie stepped off the box and shoved it beneath the podium. She flashed her winning smile, strode toward Sol, reached up to him as he bent down, and kissed him sweetly on the cheek. Calmly she whispered in his ear, "Don't blow it, you drunken idiot!"

Sol crossed to the podium and saw Normie Zee sitting in the first row. He looked at the packed house and there, at tenth-row center, were the teleprompters that carried every word of his prepared text.

Sol saw the teleprompter begin to scroll, and then he noticed Katy, sitting in the second row off to the left. Her presence only increased the jitters. But she graciously smiled to him, as if genuinely concerned that he was back to his old self, even though his old self was hardly someone she approved of.

Sol smiled weakly at her and began reading the text, trying to make it as natural-sounding as possible. "First of all, in the words of the great atheist humorist Mark Twain, 'Reports of my death have been greatly exaggerated.'"

The words on the teleprompter blurred as they scrolled down in front of him. They read, *I was clinically dead for four minutes, according to my physician...*

Sol just looked at the words, trying to make them stop blurring up. The teleprompter operator wisely stopped the crawl so Sol could catch up.

"I was clinically dead for four minutes, according to my physician..."

The teleprompter resumed the crawl, and Sol read the words.

"...And during that time, I can assure you, I heard no church bells, saw no heavenly hosts, no pearly gates..."

Sol felt the flop sweat streaming down his back, making his shirt cling to him, dripping down his forehead. He felt like Albert Brooks in *Broadcast News*.

This was it. The big shot at the anchor job. And the world had just become a sauna.

"...And during that time..." Sol read, the words continuing to blur and his delivery becoming ever more wooden, "...And during that time, I can assure you...uhhh, I can assure...no, uhh, church bells, saw no heavenly..."

The audience began to blur, and the stage felt like it had a pitch and roll to it, like a small boat out too far beyond the shore on a stormy night.

His eyes attempted to focus on the words on the tele-prompter.

...I heard no heavenly voice. I saw no dear departed relatives welcoming me into a fairytale heaven...

Sol gripped the podium, trying to make the room stop turning.

"I heard no...well, that's not exactly true..."

He could no longer make out the words on the teleprompt-er. He realized that his contact lenses were drying out on his eyes. It didn't seem fair. Fluid was pouring from every orifice on his body, but his eyes were dry? And he simply couldn't make out the words.

He peeled off the contact lenses and pulled out his glasses, squinting through them, trying to continue.

"I saw no dear..." he said. "I saw no...well, it wasn't a fairy-tale..." He was hyperventilating. His chest was heaving, and he felt like an eight-hundred-pound gorilla was camped out on top of it. He stopped trying to read the teleprompter and stepped from behind the podium, moving not toward the au-dience, but toward Katy.

"I know what I saw. I mean, I..."

He looked down at Katy, who was rising out of her seat, knowing he was in trouble. She started making her way toward him. And for some reason, instead of being reassuring, this act of compassion made him start to cry.

"Katy, I saw our son, I saw our son."

He heard the ripple of amazement coming up from the audience toward him and he felt nausea rising up.

"I saw my boy...I saw Davey...and it was so beautiful and—"

Suddenly, he fell off the apron of the stage, hitting his head on the way down on the armrest of one of the seats. He was shivering uncontrollably in a full-blown panic attack. Some idiot was above him, filming the whole thing on his cell phone to sell to the evening news. Suddenly, there were dozens of cell phones out, but nobody to help him...Except Katy, who pushed the vultures aside like a mama bear protecting her cub.

"It's going to be okay," she said, cradling his head. She looked up at one of the vultures with the iPhones and commanded in a voice that promised murder if her order was not complied with, "Call 9-1-1 or I'll shove that phone down your throat!"

The man just looked at her.

"DO IT!" she shouted like a marine drill sergeant, and the would-be TMZ reporter fumbled with his phone, turned off the camera, pulled up the keypad, and finally dialed 9-1-1.

Within minutes, Sol was on his way to New York Presbyterian for the second time in little over a week.

CHAPTER 10

The symptoms normally associated with panic attacks include hyperventilation, in which the individual thus affected may experience the feeling of an inability to get enough oxygen into their lungs. This manifestation can produce in some victims the feeling that they are about to die of asphyxiation.

A second symptom associated with panic attacks is a pronounced feeling of dizziness. More than lightheadedness, or even a sense of disequilibrium, it can manifest itself in a total loss of balance and, in some cases, vertigo.

Thus, an individual suffering from a panic attack may go from an inability to breathe to a total lack of balance and a feeling of complete disorientation, bringing about total collapse.

This can be complicated by the immediate onset of tunnel vision, resulting from loss of blood flow to the brain, to those other, more crucial sites in the body coping with the anxiety attack.

That, in turn, may lead to a feeling of tightness in the chest, nausea, profuse sweating, and paresthesia—what is commonly known as the discomfiting feeling of pins and needles, or the sensation of limbs falling asleep.

Taken together, all of these symptoms can lead a person experiencing them to believe that they are suffering a major heart attack and that they are about to die.

The feeling of impending death can, quite obviously, exacerbate the problem, creating a sense of fight or flight, in which the individual struggling with the symptoms of the panic attack may be less than cooperative with those trying to assist them.

In certain extreme cases, this can bring about a certain disassociation with reality in which everything seems unreal. This may express itself in a total withdrawal from the external world into one's own self, and behavior that seems to others to have no relation to reality. Indeed, talking to an individual suffering through such an experience is unlikely to bring forth any satisfying response, causing those attempting to treat the individual to assume that he or she is not only experiencing what appears to be an imminently fatal heart attack, but the onset of shock...or has gone completely nuts.

All of these things, taken together, can produce in the individual experiencing them a pronounced change, or what may be regarded as eccentric behavior.

For instance, the insistence that the individual in question may indeed have tought dey taw a puddy tat.

Once that occurs, fear and paranoia inevitably begin to play a part, along with a sense of self-loathing and atypical social disposition. That is then usually accompanied by a change in libidinous feelings and a tendency toward substance abuse, which, in turn, can bring the victim to thoughts of self-harm, altered sleeping habits such as insomnia, and massive mood swings, all of which can be exacerbated by the very substances or medications prescribed to bring relief of other symptoms.

It was safe to say that Doctor Sol Harkens was experiencing all of the above during his panic attack at the Jewel Box Theatre.

EMTs were called and responded with admirable alacrity.

Doctor Harkens, however, experienced mood swings, from the feeling of an imminent onset of death to advanced paranoia, altered states of reality in which figures voiced by Mel Blanc and the supporting cast of *The Simpsons* played central roles in voicing the themes that seemed to be on a loop running through his brain. In addition to Tweety Bird's obsession with puddy tats, Sol heard, over and over again, the voice of Homer Simpson constantly saying, "Beeeer...aaaagggghhhh-hh..." and "Mmmmmm...valiuuuuuum..."

He was completely uncooperative with the EMTs, who found it necessary to strap him down to the gurney as they took him on the now-familiar path to New York Presbyterian.

At that point, Sol began laughing hysterically. Katy, who had accompanied Sol into the ambulance, asked why he was laughing.

"For an atheist, it just seems to me that I'm spending an inordinate amount of time with Presbyterians."

So as not to agitate him any further, Katy began to recite her favorite Psalms of comfort inwardly to herself.

I will lift up my eyes to the mountains, from whence cometh my help

My help cometh from the LORD, who made heaven and earth.

He will not suffer thy foot to be moved: He that keepeth thee will not slumber

The LORD shall preserve thee from all evil, He shall preserve thy soul

The LORD shall preserve thy going out and thy coming in, From this time forth, and even for evermore.

And then Katy made what she realized immediately was an obvious mistake. She said aloud the word, "Amen."

"AMEN!" Sol shouted out. "SHE'S PRAYING!!! And you have *me* in restraints?! We're riding with the madwoman of Chaillot and *I'm* the one you've got strapped down to the gurney?!"

It was at that point that the reality of Doctor Sol Harkens shifted momentarily into that of the motion picture *The Big Lebowski*.

He was Walter Sobchak, and Katy assumed the role of Smokey, his competitor in what he correctly identified as a league game, which would determine who would go into the next round robin. Thus, for no apparent reason, Doctor Harkens shouted out, "OVER THE LINE, SMOKEY!"

"Sol," said Katy, as sweetly as she could, "there's nobody here named Smokey."

"*The Big Lebowski*," said one of the EMTs.

Indeed, it was, and Sol sank deep into Coen Brothers mire. "This is bowling, Katy," he said to his ex-wife. "It isn't Vietnam. There are rules."

"Sol, I don't know what you are talking about."

"*The Big Lebowski*," said the EMT, sounding not unlike Donnie saying, "I am the walrus," which only reinforced the logic to Sol Harkens, who knew subconsciously that Steve Buscemi, the actor who portrayed Donnie in *The Big Lebowski,* had been, like the EMT, a firefighter, thus reinforcing the reality of his newfound identity of Walter Sobchak.

"You're entering a world of pain, Smokey," he said to Katy, withdrawing in his mind an imaginary .45 automatic from a nonexistent bowling bag.

"I don't understand," said Katy.

"*The Big Lebowski*," repeated the EMT.

"HAS THE WHOLE WORLD GONE CRAZY?!" Sol shouted. "AM I THE ONLY ONE WHO CARES ABOUT THE RULES AROUND HERE?! MARK IT ZERO!"

"Mark what zero?" Katy asked, on the verge of tears.

"*The Big Lebowski*," said the EMT again. "He thinks he's John Goodman."

Sol turned to the EMT, suddenly realizing they were on the same wavelength. "It's a league game! Am I wrong?"

"No," said the EMT.

"Am I wrong?!" Sol demanded, doing a very passable John Goodman.

"No," responded the EMT.

"Okay, then," said Sol, temporarily mollified. "Mark it zero."

"Just say, 'Zero it is'!" the EMT whispered to Katy.

"Zero it is," Katy complied.

And Sol Harkens replaced in the bowling bag of his mind the .45 automatic he had just drawn, cocked, and pointed at Smokey to emphasize the world of pain he was about to enter. Thus pacified, he looked at Katy and said, as if it explained everything, "It's a league game."

Just as quickly as the laughter came and went, the visage of his dead son returned. His firstborn son, in whom he had poured all his fatherly devotion, smiled at his daddy with such ethereal joy that Sol, in complete desperation, broke down, inconsolably, the straps holding him to the gurney as his whole body was wracked by guttural sobs. Defeated, Harkens confessed that he wished he had died in the car accident instead of being pulled away from their sweet Davey, to all of which Katy said, fighting back tears of her own, "It's going to be all right, Sol. It's going to be all right."

By the time Norm, Tracee, and Sylvie finally arrived at New York Presbyterian, Sol had already been examined, sedated, and transferred to a private suite. They rushed frantically into the ER bay, only to be denied entrance by the security guard on duty.

"I'm sorry," the security guard greeted them, "but hospital regulations allow only one visitor in the ER."

"But I'm his agent!" exclaimed Normie Zee with unassailable logic.

"And I believe that his wife is in with him, so that makes one visitor," said the immovable security guard.

"She is his ex-wife!" Norm shouted to the heavens. "I am his current agent! What about that do you not understand?!"

The security guard got a steely-eyed Clint Eastwood look in his eyes, dropped his voice to a Dirty Harry Callahan rasp, and informed the impertinent agent, "Just about the same part that you understand about the word 'no.'"

Sol and Katy were alone in the VIP hospital suite, awaiting the head of neurology. Sol had responded well to the medication and was no longer in restraints. He no longer believed that he was Walter Sobcek or that his ex-wife Katy was his bowling competitor, the much put-upon, fragile former pacifist known only as Smokey.

"You were really nuts in the ambulance," Katy told him.

"I thought I was Walter Sobcek?"

"I don't know who you thought you were. I never saw the movie."

"You never saw *The Big Lebowski*?" asked Sol incredulously.

"I think it's a guy movie," Katy shrugged off the film flippantly.

"It's, like, one of the greatest movies ever made!"

"The EMT seemed to think so, too. He kept saying something about the fact that he was the walrus."

"*Everybody's* seen *The Big Lebowski*!" Sol still couldn't believe what he was hearing. How could he have spent years with someone who had never seen The Dude?

"I really think it's a guy movie."

Thankfully, a female doctor in her late forties, wearing a white lab coat and carrying the hateful iPad instead of the metal-covered chart, entered the VIP suite, interrupting the inquisition.

"I'm Doctor Lakshmi Patel, Chief of Neurology, and a very big fan of yours, Doctor Harkens."

Katy rolled her eyes, and Sol smiled appreciatively.

"I'm halfway through *Aborting God*," Doctor Patel said, "and I love it."

Katy began to wish she could retreat into the world of *The Big Lebowski*, herself. Bowling seemed more pleasurable than hearing another fan fawning over her ex-husband.

"I'm glad you're enjoying it," said Sol, smiling a somewhat stoned grin.

Doctor Patel scrolled through Sol's iPad chart and then looked up, smiling. "Well," she said, "the good news is, looking at your CT scans and MRI, the clot hasn't moved at all. It hasn't broken up and traveled. And, it's not pushing against anything that could've caused this episode you just had."

"Then what was it?"

"He was acting pretty goofy," Katy said.

"Goofy in what way?" Doctor Patel asked, a concerned expression on her face.

"It was something about somebody named...Liebowitz?"

"Lebowski," Sol corrected. "*The Big Lebowski.*"

"Ah," said Doctor Patel. "'The Dude abides.'"

"He does, indeed," agreed Sol.

Doctor Patel turned to Katy. "Mrs. Harkens, your husband—"

"*Ex*-husband," Katy said.

"Ah," said Doctor Patel.

"We're divorced," Katy added, though it was clear.

"Amicably," said Sol. "I mean, if she was going off to Hawaii with her boyfriend, Marty Ackerman, I'm not saying I'd watch the Pomeranian, even if he *had* papers, but—"

Katy looked at Sol. "I have no idea what you just said."

"It's a reference to *The Big Lebowski*," Doctor Patel told her helpfully. "You really should see it." She turned to Sol. "Look. You've experienced a terrible trauma. It isn't unusual to have anxiety, sleeplessness, migraines, depression—a myriad of symptoms, including panic attacks, which can bring with them hallucinations, altered states of reality—all of the things you've experienced."

"I kept hearing Homer Simpson in my head too."

"Obviously the lecture tonight was very stressful to you. My advice would be to avoid putting yourself in those kinds of stressful situations. Now, I'm sure you have some questions for me."

"What drugs can you give me?"

"Well," said Doctor Patel, "there are many alternatives to medications. Yoga, meditation—"

"I want drugs."

"You should listen to what Doctor Patel says," Katy interceded. "Meditation—"

"Meditation takes forever. Drugs are quick," Sol explained, as if he were schooling them on something so obvious a six-year-old could understand.

"Everything isn't about instant gratification," Katy said.

"Trust me, when you're suffering from a panic attack, that's exactly what you want. Instant isn't soon enough!"

"That's very true," Doctor Patel conceded. "The attacks can be very frightening. I can prescribe Zoloft."

"It lessens the libido." Sol turned to Katy. "No offense." He turned back to Patel. "I'd rather not have my libido lessened."

"I can prescribe Wellbutrin, which is an NDRI. It's one of the few antidepressants not frequently associated with libidinous side effects."

"My kind of drug," Sol smiled.

"Doctor Patel, my husband has been known to be a substance abuser."

Katy's concern was clear however, Sol was not about to have his former wife take away his only hope for relief.

"But I won't this time. Scout's honor," he promised.

"It shouldn't be mixed with alcohol," explained Doctor Patel.

"Absolutely not," said Sol. "That's not going to be a problem, whatsoever."

"And it should only be taken as prescribed."

"To the letter," said Sol, suddenly the best Boy Scout in the room.

"And," added Patel, "it shouldn't be mixed with any other prescription medications."

"The last thing I would ever do," said Sol.

"Why do they always fall for this?" asked Katy, looking toward the heavens.

Doctor Patel wrote out a prescription and handed it to Sol. "Here's the prescription. Thirty-day supply, non-refillable. And my professional suggestion is total rest and avoidance of any stress."

"Absolutely," said Sol.

"Now," said Doctor Patel. "Was there anything else you'd like to ask?"

"Not that I can think of," said Sol.

"Yes, there was, Sol!" Katy egged him on. "Ask her! Go ahead and ask her. This is your chance."

Sol took the opportunity, hoping for a rational explanation even though he had not found one himself. "Sometimes," he began, "when people have a near-death experience, they talk about seeing things, you know, the tunnel of light, the heavenly chorus..."

Doctor Patel put down her electronic chart, walked over, and sat down on the edge of Sol's bed. She had an excellent bedside manner that was, in itself, immediately comforting. "It's called the 'death surge,'" she told him. "Often, when someone almost dies, there is a surge of brain activity, which would be like all of the neurons firing at once, that gives them the intense sense of seeing or even experiencing something. They aren't actually experiencing it, but they believe they are. The truth, however, is they are only seeing their imaginations literally running wild. Did you experience something like that, Doctor Harkens?"

Sol looked away from Katy, avoiding any kind of eye contact, then looked at Doctor Patel. "No, nothing like that. Thank you, Doctor."

"Not at all." She got up, retrieved her iPad medical chart, and headed out of the room, stopping at the door as though she had forgotten something. "One last, little thing."

"What is it?" Sol asked.

Doctor Lakshmi Patel blushed like a young undergraduate student with a crush on her professor. "Would you mind taking a selfie with me?"

Katy, yet again, rolled her eyes to the heavens.

It took almost another hour to sign the paperwork to get Sol released and his prescription for Wellbutrin fulfilled. Then he and Katy hailed a cab and made their way through the post-theater traffic down to the Village.

Katy helped an exhausted Sol into his apartment.

"Did what Doctor Patel said put your mind at rest?" Katy asked.

"Look who you're talking to," Sol responded as he placed the Wellbutrin on the kitchen counter. "The World's Most Famous Atheist. So, if my neurons are gonna surge, what I see is gonna look like the grotto at Hef's on New Year's Eve. On steroids! I've done acid. Trust me, I know what my hallucinations look like. He was so beautiful, Katy," he said, in a tone of voice Katy had never heard before. "He looked so at peace. And so happy. God, I wish I had died with him."

"And I thank God you didn't," Katy said, touching Sol's arm.

There was an awkwardness to it that they both felt, and slowly, she pulled her fingers away, and as she did, Sol felt, strangely, like a boat cut loose from its moorings. They were suddenly both bashful as seventh graders.

"Alright. I...I'll check on you tomorrow," she told him.

"There's no need to," Sol said, hating the feeling of self-pity that was beginning to wash over him.

"I need to," Katy said. "Okay?"

Sol looked at her. It was amazing that the sight of her, the feel of her that close in the room, could still have the same effect on him, even after all the bitterness of their divorce. "Thank you. I appreciate it."

There was the awkwardness again. She wanted to kiss his cheek but didn't want it to be misconstrued. Instead, she simply said, "Good night. Get some rest," and walked past the posters of Sol's God-bashing books toward the door.

"Sure thing," Sol said, as he watched the door close behind her.

He turned around and looked at his uber-hip loft. It was every bachelor's dream. And tonight, it was cold as Siberia. And as the song said, empty as a poor boy's pocket with nothing to lose.

Sol picked up the Wellbutrin from the kitchen counter and crossed to the bar. He pulled out a bottle of vodka and poured himself a large shot, popped the Wellbutrin into his mouth, and just to make sure he got some sleep, threw in a couple diazepam for good measure. Then he took another drink and said to the empty apartment, "Hi, hon. I'm home."

CHAPTER 11

"How's Dad doing?" Gus asked.

He had his mother's angelic eyes and dark good looks, but there was that hint of a lisp that he carried, perhaps genetically, from his father. That was the thing that drove Katy crazy, that made her want to hug and kiss, squeeze and protect forever her precious boy, her sweet Gus, with his oh-so-serious manner that, despite his best efforts, reminded her so much of both her husband and her own grandfather. There was an old-soul seriousness there. You couldn't bulldoze this boy. You couldn't even try.

Katy was checking her lipstick in the mirror by the door, preparing to leave, when Gus had appeared beside her with his question.

There was nothing casual about it. Nothing reminiscent of "How's it going? How's your Aunt Tilly? How are the rosebushes?" There was a somberness there and, indeed, an inherent warning.

Amazing, Katy thought. *All he has to do is say three words "How's Dad doing?"—and he has me on the ropes. I'm playing defense. He's the adult, and I'm the child.*

It was not a position she relished, nor, if truth be told, even accepted for a moment with any degree of grace.

He was *her* child, not the other way around. "How's Dad doing?" meant, "What are you Doing, going over to the man who abandoned us? How dare you set us all up to be hurt by him once again?" That's what "How's Dad doing?" really meant. She loved him for it—and resented it at the same time.

Her mind raced for as noncommittal an answer as she could find. No White House spin doctor had ever searched more fervently for an answer that meant absolutely nothing.

Question: "What did the President know, and when did he know it?"

White House spin doctor: "Well, as you know, the President has a rather large daily agenda, which places him at the forefront of the leadership of the free world in areas of economics, foreign policy, and domestic concerns. At any given point in time, I cannot tell you what he may know about any given subject unless there's more specificity to your question. I should think that would be axiomatic, wouldn't you?"

Thus, Katy replied to Gus's query of "How's Dad doing?" by saying, "He's been through a lot, you know?"

Gus saw through it quicker than Mike Wallace on the best day he ever had. He decided against taking the bait, and cut straight to the chase. He looked at her with those brown doe eyes that seemed to have two millennia of all that life has to offer behind them. "You're spending a lot of time with him," he said, fixing his gaze upon her. Then he dropped the hammer. "What's up with that?"

Katy was a teenager once again, and her father was querying her about the useless bad boy to whom she had become attracted. With her father, though, the guilt was limited to, "How can you do this to your own reputation, let alone our whole family's?" But Gus's heat-seeking missile carried a much greater payload than that. It included the very pointed accusation, "How can you put my brother and me through the narcissistic, alcohol-and-drug-induced meat grinder known as our father again?"

Katy reeled back, like George Foreman suddenly being hit by a reinvigorated Muhammad Ali who was slipping off the ropes one second and miraculously landing left-right combinations another after absorbing eight rounds of body blows. She was as stunned as Foreman, operating now not out of intellect, but instinct.

She fell back, as boxers do, on the most reliable gift she had. For George Foreman, it was the greatest stiff left jab in the history of boxing. For Katy, and every other mother who walked the face of the earth, it was guilt.

"How can you ask a question like that?" she said. "He's hurting, Gus, and he's scared."

Gus slipped past Katy's left jab of guilt as easily as the great Ali slipped a punch by a fighter who did not know he was already defeated. "And what happens when he's better?" Again, like the great Ali, that was a feint. And he didn't wait on her to follow up. He landed a right behind his own left jab, and it was a vicious one. It took no prisoners. It allowed its quarry no quarter. It went straight for the solar plexus, and was meant to do one thing: knock the air out of you, so you couldn't breathe. Thus, when Gus said, "What happens when he gets better?" he followed it up with, "He's gonna dump you again."

There it is. Five words that spoke volumes. *He dumped you once, or don't you remember? Or do you want to remember? Or are you lying to yourself? Are you enabling a narcissistic addict as you did once before? Or are you abandoning your responsibility as a mother to protect your children against any danger they may face, even if it comes from their own father? From the man you loved. From the man who your children know you love still? Who have heard your unanswered prayers for his salvation, ever since they were capable of the notion of memory?* That's what "He's gonna dump you again" meant.

He knew it.

She knew it.

Each of them knew exactly what he had meant.

The challenge was on the table and could not lay unanswered.

Katy tried to fall back on what she deemed adult logic. If she could not win on the merits of the case, she would settle for a technicality. "We're not back together," she said, looking evenly into Gus's eternal eyes. "So how can he dump me?"

Gus shifted his weight like a boxer getting ready to load up on his punch, the kind that starts with all your weight on one foot and then carries up, through the canvas, all the way up your legs and into your spine, until one is leaning full force into what has to be a knockout. As long as your opponent sees it coming.

"I don't trust him, Mom," Gus said. And here came the punch. Off the canvas, through his leg, up into his spine, and into a right hook. The ultimate truth that Gus knew about his father, and knew in the marrow of his bones. "He's a user, Mom. He uses you, he uses Connor, and he uses me."

Katy could do nothing more now than cover up, arms in front of her face, trying to shield herself from the blows, trying to stay on her feet, though what Gus said had sent her reeling, and the only thing that kept her from being knocked out was that she knew it was coming.

"That's not true!" she said, and there was something of the little girl in her voice, of the child appealing to the parent, of the child pleading, "Why are you saying this to me? Why would you hurt me in this way?"

"He loves you guys," she told Gus, "and you know it." Translation: *How can you doubt my love for you, no matter what I do?* "Why are you saying all this to me?" And truly, here, she was the child, appealing to the parent in Gus, begging him to hurt her no further.

And, knowing how much he had hurt her, Gus appealed to the logical parent inside of her. "It's because I don't want to see you get hurt again."

And that gave Katy her opening to strike back with a knock-out truth of her own. "You don't want to see *me* get hurt," she asked, "or you're afraid you might get hurt?"

Like two spent boxers leaning on each other's shoulders, there was no more fight left in either of them, as Gus simply replied, "Both."

And the unspoken truth between them was that Sol wasn't even in the room, and yet, it was he who had inflicted the wounds. They were fighting ghosts. The ghost of unspoken and unacknowledged grief for Katy's firstborn and Gus's big brother, and the ghost of Gus's father and Katy's former husband, who, as they flailed in the waters of their own sorrow, had paddled away in a life raft made of alcohol and drugs and self-pity.

<hr />

Though it was only late afternoon, not even yet early evening, Sol was passed out drunk on his deep leather sofa. He had no idea how long he'd been unconscious. He had a vague memory of a one o'clock newscast on the twenty-four-hour news station still playing in the background.

He had a vague memory of pills taken, alcohol consumed, and tears shed.

He had a vague memory of grief, and guilt, of the bile of acid reflux made up of vodka and narcotics and stale corn chips. He had felt the acid in his throat before the sound of the buzzer at his door ripped through his body like a chainsaw.

First, there was the acid in his throat and the thought that he was about to vomit. Then came the noise, like that chainsaw ripping through green wood, until he realized it was the buzzer at the door. It jolted him awake, like a pair of battery cables applied by a skilled Taliban interrogator to the more sensitive parts of one's anatomy.

He leaped up from the couch as if from electric shock and suddenly remembered he had a doorman.

The doorman was supposed to be the guardian, the offensive lineman who sacrificed his body to allow him, Sol Harkens, undoubtedly the quarterback of his own team, a few seconds in the pocket to get the pass off before being tackled by Lawrence Taylor or William "The Refrigerator" Perry. He was the Praetorian Guard, there to lay down his life for Sol's Caesar.

And yet, there was that buzzer, ripping through his brain yet again.

Instead of getting up off the couch like a normal human being, Sol vaulted over the back for no apparent reason, other than to snatch up the bottle of vodka that stood waiting on the shelf beneath the poster of his visage.

The vault over the back of the couch was the shortest distance between him and the drink, which he instinctively hoped would ease the pain of the incessant buzzing, which his miserable excuse for a doorman had failed to prevent.

"Alright! Alright! Yeah, yeah, yeah. I'm comin'! Keep your pants on!" He snatched the bottle of vodka, fortified himself with a swallow, and felt the alcohol going down fight the acid reflux coming up in his throat.

"I mean, what do I even have a doorman *for*, anyway?! Why don't we just forget about it?! 'Why don't we go up to Sol's place? I mean, he's got booze, he's got pills, let's have a party!'"

So saying, he flung the door open, ready to do battle with whomever had dared to intrude upon his stupor.

"Kate!" he said, recognizing his ex-wife instantly. Then, without another word, he turned on his heel, left the door open to her, and stumbled back into his apartment.

"You're drunk?!" she demanded.

Sol braced himself against the wall, which seemed to rush at him, knocking one of his posters of himself akimbo. "Can't pull the wool over your eyes," he said, acknowledging Katy's observation. "But, in truth, I think it's not so much the vodka as it is the pain pills. Or maybe it's the vodka *and* the pain pills."

Sol lurched for the security of the sofa while Katy stopped at the pile of boxes stacked up against the usually Zen-like sparseness of the walls in Sol's apartment.

"What's in all these boxes?" she asked with genuine curiosity.

Well, here was a nonconfrontational subject, and Sol latched onto it immediately.

"Wipe-Wowies," he informed her, carefully enunciating every syllable, and with no small amount of pride in his newly acquired possessions.

Katy just looked at him.

People who are in long-standing relationships don't need to ask questions; they just need to throw *that look*. This look, in particular, meant, "What can this idiot possibly be talking about?"

Sol turned back toward her and, by way of explanation, said, "Wipe-Wowies. You know? You can't sleep, it's three in the morning, you're sittin' there, zonked out in front of the TV, and that carnival guy comes on..." He said it with a certain sense of awe, as if relating the fact that a genie had emerged, completely uninvited, from his television. The box atop the stack had already been opened, and he pulled out a chamois-like cloth, holding the near-miraculous object for her inspection. "Did you know that these can soak up two hundred times their weight in liquid? It's a proven, scientific fact. So I ordered six cases."

Katy just shook her head.

For his part, Sol raised the bottle to take another swig.

"Give me the vodka," she said, in a tone that was not to be trifled with.

Ever the gracious host, Sol said, "You want a drink? I'll pour you one!"

"No," Katy said, grabbing the bottle out of his hand. "I don't want a drink. And I won't stay here if you are drinking. You're the one who invited me, pal," she said, totally ignoring the fact that she said she'd come by to check up on *him*. "You're the one who said you needed to talk!"

Sol felt himself listing noticeably, and knew that he would not make it to the safety of the sofa. And so he pirouetted, not, he noted to himself, without a small amount of grace, to one of the director's chairs that sat along the breakfast bar of his kitchen.

"Well," Katy continued, crossing into the kitchen. "I don't talk to drunks."

"You oughtta try it sometime," Sol slurred. "Some of my best friends are drunks."

"Not this time," Katy said, pouring his bottle of vodka down the drain.

Sol winced, as if a blade had been inserted into his solar plexus and twisted.

"That," he said, "is Potocki vodka. Almost impossible to come by in this country. It is the same vodka served at Dukes Bar in London, where Sir Ian Fleming created the Bond martini. And that's what you're pouring down my drain."

"Can't pull the wool over your eyes," Katy retorted with a certain smugness in her eyes, shaking out the last few drops.

"Ah, Kate. Bonny Kate. Prettiest Kate in Christendom. Thy beauty doth make me like thee well. Thou must be married to no man but me, for I am he 'twas born to tame you, Kate..." Sol panicked slightly and added, "That's not a proposal. Just a little Shakespeare."

"*The Taming of the Shrew*?" Katy asked.

"If memory serves," said Sol, trying to remember if there was another bottle of Potocki vodka closer than the bar at the end of the living room, a distance he knew he could not safely traverse.

"And I'm the shrew?!" Katy demanded. "I am so out of here."

She crossed around the breakfast bar, heading out of the kitchen, but Sol strategically pivoted his director's chair to block her path.

"No, honestly," he said. "Please. Really. Really. Truly. Honestly. I need to talk."

"You've got a shrink," Katy said, trying to get around him. "That's what you pay him for."

Sol took her by the arms, not unaware of the slight feeling of electricity that passed between them every time they touched.

"Katy," he said, "nobody but you would understand what I'm saying. I can't sleep. I can't think. I can't not think. I can't stop thinking about how he looked and how it felt and what he said!"

Sol felt he needed something sturdier beneath him than the director's chair. He walked past Katy to the womb-like safety of the leather sofa. Knowing that if he flopped onto it, he would vomit, he eased into its familiar and comforting contours.

"What who said?" Katy crossed into the living room and sat next to him.

Sol looked her in the eyes.

"Davey," Sol said. "I saw our son, Katy."

"What are you talking about?"

"There was this voice," Sol recounted, remembering the tunnel, the softness of his boy's skin, the little arms around his neck. "And it said that it wasn't my time, and then Davey said, 'Daddy. Let there be light.' And I felt myself being pulled back, away from our boy, away from this...this...unbelievable feeling of love and peace, and I didn't want to come back! I wanted to just take him in my arms, you know? And he said it again. 'Let there be light, Daddy.' And I sit here, night after night..."

Sol was fighting back tears now. There was no vestige of the great and arrogant Sol Harkens. In his place was a man devastated by sadness and longing for death. His vanity destroyed by his inner turmoil. He clenched his fists, utterly and completely helpless against the unending pain of his son's death.

"And, honest-to-God, I have no idea what to do with that! Let there be light. LTBL. LTBL...and I feel like any second, I'm gonna grab every pill I can find and take them all, just to get back to him or, if not that, just to end the pain." He tried to breathe and a sob broke free from him instead.

Katy had never seen him like this. Truth be told, she had never seen anyone like this, anyone so totally bereft, so devoid of hope, so completely alone. She knew that there was a very real chance that, right now, if she left, he would indeed do exactly what he said, and she didn't know where all the pills were, so they couldn't be flushed down the drain like the vodka.

She chose her words as carefully as she had ever chosen any in her life. "Sol, you know, you've gotten the best scientific explanations, and they haven't satisfied you. They haven't brought you any comfort. The only thing you have to show for it is six cases of Wipe-Wowies."

The two of them managed a slight, intimate laugh. And then, Sol confessed. "I bought a dozen Miracle Mops too."

Katy laughed out loud. "Well, praise Jesus! You'll allow the notion of a miracle, when it comes to mops at least."

Sol now spoke sincerely about the miraculous nature of the items he had bought from the three a.m. electronic carnival barker who emerged, genie-like, from his television set in the dark nights of his soul. He spoke in awe, if not in reverence. "You can take the head off and put it in the washing machine. It's made of nine thousand continuous strands woven together. I wouldn't pooh-pooh that mop."

"Would you consider consulting another source? I mean, you've tried Dr. Patel and late-night TV."

Their heads were close together now. It was as intimate as they had been since before their divorce.

"Let me guess," said Sol, who was longing for a cool sip of frozen Potocki vodka. "Your pastor?"

"What have you got to lose?" Katy asked, no judgement whatsoever in her voice.

"Katy, I don't know. I don't know anything anymore. If I could just get some sleep..."

He was totally and completely exhausted. This intimidating man, whose strength she had always taken for granted.

"Let me hold you," she said softly. "You'll sleep then."

"Katy," Sol said, with just a hint of the mischief in his eye that used to drive her absolutely crazy. "I appreciate the offer, but honestly, I'm just not in the mood."

"That's not what I'm offering," Katy said, unable to hold back a smile. "I said I'll hold you, and I will. And that's all I'll do. And then you'll sleep."

They moved as one, Sol leaning over toward her lap and Katy cradling him with her arm and putting her hand beneath his forehead, as if he were but a babe. The feel of her lap was the most familiar thing in the world to Sol, as if he were home once again, and for the moment, he was safe.

"Kate," he muttered. "Bonny Kate. Prettiest Kate in Christendom..."

And with that, his head in her lap, with her hand stroking his forehead, he was instantly asleep. Katy held him, not moving, hearing only in her mind Gus's words and her reply.

He's going to dump you again, Gus had said.

We're not back together, she had answered, *so how can he dump me?*

And as those words echoed in her mind, she stroked Sol's hair and fought back the tears she felt welling up in her eyes.

Kevin Sorbo as Sol with Gary Grubbs as Dr. Fournier

Olivia Fox as Vanessa Bietchevskaya

Sol hugs Davey

Kevin Sorbo as Sol Harkens and Michael Franzese as Pastor Vinny

Katy and Sol

Braeden and Shane Sorbo as Gus and Connor Harkens

Dionne Warwick playing herself

Donielle Artese as Tracee

Sean Hannity playing himself

A family that works together... Shane, Sam, Kevin and Braeden Sorbo

The Let There Be Light *app performs!*

CHAPTER 12

Sol Harkens sat at his usual table—in the back, near the kitchen— at Mario's Mediterranean Cuisine, the former Meyer's Falafel, nursing a cup of mud-thick Turkish coffee with cardamom and one and a half teaspoons of sugar.

Little had changed in Meyer's Falafel except for a badly painted mural of a nondescript Italian port, which had once been a mural of Jaffa Port and had been badly transformed into an imitation of Positano. Or perhaps they were trying for Santa Margherita or Portofino. At any rate, what had been Arab architecture and the Andromeda Rock had seen an addition of unidentifiable mountains, terra cotta coloring, and a bad transformation of the rock that, legend proclaimed, had held the chained Andromeda into a sort of clunky-looking fishing boat, completely out of proportion to the bay in which it plied its trade. As an afterthought, someone had decided that it would be a good idea to have smoke pouring out of the mountain, thus suggesting that it might be Vesuvius. Instead, it simply looked like a grease stain that had been too high up to clean.

Mario's Mediterranean Cuisine's menu had also been slightly altered to include the addition of two mediocre pastas and the change in nomenclature from Israeli Salad to Greek Salad, the latter having been accomplished by simply adding feta cheese, cutting the cucumbers and tomatoes a little bit thicker, and adding a few more Kalamata olives.

Still, the Turkish coffee with cardamom was a far better jolt than any of the local latte joints'. It was full-strength rocket fuel, and you had to wait for the thick coffee to settle at the bottom of the small glass in which it was served. Otherwise, one's pharyngeal gag reflex would turn the otherwise, bracing experience of Turkish coffee into a sudden near-death experience.

The coffee was served in the same kind of peasant glass that Italians used to serve a basic, everyday Rosso with enough edge to stand up to any bucatini all'Amatriciana. Sol knew that when the small glass could no longer create third-degree burns on the tips of his fingers, the coffee would have settled to the bottom and now be safe to drink. It was a primitive but infallible bit of folk wisdom, which endeared Sol even more to the ceremonial nature of the serving and consumption of Meyer's, which was to say, Mario's, Turkish coffee.

The smells of fried chickpeas, pounded sesame, olive oil, fresh-cut tomatoes, and Middle Eastern spices filled the air. From the kitchen came a constant stream of what sounded like Hebrew abuse. Israeli kitchen help, it seemed, only had one decibel level, something just below full-scale riot.

But for Sol, the place, perhaps because of the noise, the laughter, the shouting, the pure, good-natured humanity of it, was comforting. Unlike his loft, it was the place where he felt connected to humanity instead of cut off from it, and Meyer never bothered him. Sol could sit with his Turkish coffee, writing for hours, if he liked. As far as Meyer was concerned, the back table was Sol's. It was the only table that had a permanent "RESERVED" sign on it.

Invariably, Sol would give in to temptation, no matter how lost he had gotten in his writing, and order up hummus with ful, which was Arabic for "beans"; large, flat, straight-from-the-oven, to-die-for, pizza-sized flatbread called laffa, a side order of falafel balls, and assorted olives and pickled vegetables: beets, radishes, cucumbers, all of them homemade, each one more delicious than the other.

It was, in fact, the place where Sol's thinking was at its clearest. In spite of being somewhat ADHD, Sol found the noise comforting rather than distracting. Besides, if he were at home instead of at Meyer's or the newly christened Mario's, he would be drinking, and he knew it. More than that, he would be drunk, whereas, it seemed, Meyer's Turkish coffee could, in a single dose, wipe out nearly all the effects of Sol's total alcohol consumption from the night before.

Sol had made his pilgrimage to what he still thought of as Meyer's Falafel to try and work through the seemingly-apocryphal message transmitted to him by his beloved son, Davey, "Let there be light."

Sol had his yellow legal pad, on which he still continued to write his literary works, disdaining computers completely for the satisfying feel of pressing the words down into the paper.

On the pad, he had written, rather like Jack Nicholson in *The Shining*, the phrase "Let there be light" over and over.

It got him absolutely nowhere.

The only place it led was, inexorably, to the memory of the immortal *Simpsons* episode in which Homer, Jack Nicholson-like, smashes an axe through a succession of doors, sticks his head through, and says, "HHHHEEEEEERE'S JOHNNY! D'OH! DAAAAAAAAAAAAAVID LLLLLEEEEEEEEEEETTTTER-MAN! *D'OH!* I'M MIKE WALLACE! I'M MORLEY SAFER!

I'M ED BRADLEY! ALL THIS AND ANDY ROONEY TO-NIGHT ON *SIXTY MINUTES*!!!"

Usually, the memory of that episode would produce cascades of laughter or, at the very least, chortles from Sol Harkens. *But*, he thought, *this is no chortling matter.*

He decided to switch tack and write "LTBL" again and again, trying to decipher the hidden message again.

He had filled half a page with the letters "LTBL" when, in frustration, he cried out, "What? LTBL! LTBL! What does it mean? Why don't you just tell me, already? Why does everything have to be a mystery?!"

It was at this point that Batya, the punked-out, nose-ringed Israeli waitress, leaned over his shoulder, invading not only his safe space but his ruminations, as Israelis are wont to do, and said, "Eet's because you got all the letter wrong."

"What are you talking about?" Sol demanded in his most stentorian tones. Indeed, he could achieve a level of patrician condescension that made John Kerry look like a Franciscan monk, none of which, however, could put a dent in a punked-out Israeli waitress's day.

Batya had, after all, been a soldier in the Caracal Batallion. She had humped forty pounds of gear and could shoot a pattern the size of a quarter with a Mini-Tavor at 250 yards. She had faced ISIS fighters across the Egyptian border. Thus, her reaction to the renowned Professor Harkens was "Stentorian, schmentorian." She couldn't care less.

She picked up the pad with hummus-stained fingers and pointed at the letters. "You got the letters all wrong," she insisted again. "Is no 'LTBL', it 'LGBT'! You the big professor and I got to tell *you*?"

"I *don't* have the letters wrong," Sol said, snatching back his legal pad. "It's 'L – T – B – L'!" He pointed at each letter for emphasis.

"LTBL," said the punked-out waitress.

"Right!" said Sol Harkens, in his most decisive tone.

"Not LGBT, like the parade, with the rainbows and the flags and all the men dressed like women?"

"No parades, no flags," said Sol. "It's LTBL."

"So, what it means?" asked Batya.

"That's what I'm trying to figure out!" Sol said, realizing he was gesticulating as much as any Israeli.

"If you don't know what it means, why you write it?"

"Because it's important to me to figure out what it *does* mean!" His exasperation was increasing.

"Okay," said Batya, "I tell you. Eet's not that complicated. Lesbian, trans, bi...lesbian!" She smiled with no small amount of satisfaction, having deciphered the code.

"Let there be light," Sol said, in a disgusted tone.

"That's what it means?" Batya asked incredulously.

"Yes!" said Sol, glad there wasn't an axe on the wall with which to break through a door of his own. "'LTBL' stands for 'Let there be light!'"

"Okay, well, there you are," she said. "Problem solved!"

There was no winning with Israelis in general, and with Batya, the punked-out, nose-pierced Israeli waitress, in particular.

Sol surrendered. In utter and complete defeat, he paid his bill and retreated to the sanctuary of his loft apartment.

The woman had, quite literally, driven him to drink. He poured a large tumbler-full of vodka and threw in a few ice cubes. In the hopes of counteracting the effects of the electronic buzz of three peasant glasses of Meyer's Turkish coffee, he popped a Xanax and a couple diazepam like M&Ms and washed them down with Tito's finest.

The man-eating, mutant-cicada-like buzz of his intercom interrupted his guzzling.

Sol took another long swallow off the vodka and crossed to the intercom on the wall, pressed the button, and in his usual charming way, said, "What."

"Doctor Harkens," said Zach, the much put-upon doorman, "your agent is on his way up."

"I don't want to see my agent! Why'd you let him—"

"I'm sorry, Doctor Harkens. He just blew right past me!"

"What's the point of having a doormat...I mean, a doorman, if—"

"It's Norm! I mean, you know Norm!"

"Yeah," said Sol, feeling like he'd just lost a debate. "I know Norm."

The doorbell rang.

"Speak of the devil," said Sol, meaning it not in the least bit metaphorically. He crossed to the door and opened it, ushering in Normie Zee, in his blue blazer, yellow tie, and matching yellow pocket square.

"Hey, pal," said Normie, in his laid-back LA tone.

"What's up, Norm? You want a drink?" Sol asked, barely masking his impatience.

"Little early in the day, pal, isn't it?"

"Not if you're in London."

"But, we're not in London."

"In that case," said Sol, "I share your confusion."

With that, Sol drained his tumbler of vodka and headed back to the bar for a refill. Norm crossed to the leather sofa and casually threw his leg up over the arm as if this his home and not Sol's.

"Pally, the other night, you went down in a heap and started breakdancing on the floor." Norm looked around on the coffee table. "You have any munchies? Those little honey-roasted peanuts? I love those things."

"Get to the point, Norm," said Sol.

"Where was I?"

"I was breakdancing on the floor."

"Exactly!" said Norm. And I can't say it wasn't entertaining, I'll grant you that, but it's hardly a way to push a book. Catch my drift?"

"I had an off day," Sol explained, taking another sip of vodka. He could feel the Xanax and diazepam setting in and the effects of the Turkish coffee sailing off into the sunset. "It happens when you've been clinically dead for four minutes."

"That's why you have me!" Norm said, getting up and crossing into the kitchen. "Maybe in one of these cupboards?"

"Maybe what's in one of those cupboards?" Sol asked, feeling the vodka hit, as well as the pain pills.

"Food, pally! You know, like a normal person? Food? Something to eat?"

"By the Wipe-Wowies, along the wall. Knock yourself out."

Norm saw five cases marked *Patriot Survival Food.* "What *is* this?!"

"I don't know. It says it's good for twenty-five years, so none of it can have gone bad. I think there's lasagna...just add hot water. I think there's a chocolate cake in there..."

"This isn't munchies, pal. This is what you put in a bomb shelter. When you're crazy. Look, the point is, it's time to get back out there. I set up an interview."

"The doctor said to avoid stressful situations."

"Look, I'm not asking you to join me and the wife for dinner. You wanna talk stressful situations? We serve Xanax for hors d'oeuvres. On the other hand, a little one-on-one interview, print media only, no cameras, for *Manhattan Style Magazine*? Puff piece. You can knock it out of the park in your sleep." He picked up a packet of dehydrated lasagna. "You say this isn't bad, huh? How long does it take to boil water, anyway?"

"I don't know, Norm, I'm not a chef! It's New York! If I need boiled water, I order out for it!"

"Can you microwave it?"

"Norm, there are directions on it. They're in English. Read them."

"It looks complicated." He shrugged his shoulders and tore open the foil packet. Norm took out a handful of broken dehydrated lasagna and put it in his mouth. "I'll tell you the truth," he said, "I've had worse. Look, kid, I gotta be honest with ya. This isn't about auditioning for any talk show gig. You already blew that the other night. This is about keeping the gig you've already got." Norm poured the contents of the packet into a bowl, put in some water, put it in the microwave, and pressed REHEAT. "Pally, I'm your best friend, and I'm talking to you like your brother. You gotta snap out of it or you're gonna tear down what you've been building for the last twenty years. You know what I mean?"

The bowl exploded.

"OK," said Norm. "So, that doesn't work."

Nighttime brought the familiar genie out from his magical box. Sol sat zonked out in front of his TV set, watching the latest carnival pitchman. Decked out in a sushi chef's bandana and what could have been David Carradine's Kung Fu gi, he was hawking the amazing Gwanzoo Knife set.

"Hi, Frankie here for the amazing Gwanzoo Knife set! It slices! It dices! Watch this! Tomatoes, sliced paper-thin! With a blade so strong, you can even cut through iron! What they wouldn't have given for *this* in Alcatraz, huh? Huh? And if you order now, you not only get the full eight-piece Gwanzoo Knife set, you also get the Chop-o-Matic! Onions make you cry? Give the Chop-o-Matic a try! Potatoes too hard to peel? The Chop-o-Matic's the real deal! And if you order now, we'll send you *two* sets of the Gwanzoo Knives and *two* Chop-o-Matics for only *three easy payments* of thirty-nine-ninety-five!"

For the second time that day, Sol felt exactly like Homer Simpson. There was only one thought that went through his brain. *Must. Have. Gwanzoomatic.*

Somewhere between that thought and his alarm going off the next morning, Sol had evidently bought ten sets of the amazing Gwanzoo Knives and accompanying Chop-o-Matics.

He searched for the alarm that wouldn't stop ringing, found it, and threw it against the wall. Then he stumbled into the shower, popped an upper, poured in the Visine, and dressed in his most casual slacks and sweater to hide the fact that the very thought of a reporter coming into his domain was bringing on a full-blown panic attack. He self-medicated with a couple shots of vodka until the giant man-eating cicada-like buzzer shot through his brain.

It was Zach the Doormat apologizing for the fact that Norm had just blown by him once again. There wasn't even a ring at the doorbell this time. Sol had forgotten to lock the door, and Norm, like a very laid-back Kramer, simply walked in.

"Hey, pal."

"Morning, Norm," Sol said, as if greeting an undertaker.

"Doctor Sol Harkens, Cat Ryerson, from *Manhattan Style*."

Sol checked her up and down, despite himself. In a normal situation, he would have made a play for her, but he had long ago left normal behind. He felt the sweat start rolling down the back of his shirt. "Come on in. Have a seat. Can I get you anything?"

"No, I'm fine," Cat said, taking out her notebook. She eased herself onto the leather couch. "Shall we get right to it?"

"Sure, why not?" Sol sat across from her at what he thought was a respectable distance, though he kept wondering whether he was too close.

"The other night—"

"I had a full-blown panic attack," he said, before she could go any further.

"And how are you feeling now?"

"Dandy. If you were there, I hope you got a refund."

"You seemed," said Cat, "to go into that panic attack as you were talking about what you experienced during the time that you were clinically dead."

Sol could feel his skin going clammy and sweat beading on his forehead. "Could be. I really don't remember." He could feel his facial features pulling into a feigned hangdog smile as he shook his head.

"During that time you were clinically dead, did you actually get a glimpse of the great beyond?" She leaned in toward him. The smell of her perfume was making him nauseous. Or the shots and pills. Or all of the above.

"I...I...I really don't know."

"Well, let me put it a different way," Cat said, leaning in closer. "Now that you've experienced whatever it was that you experienced, did it change you in any way? Your outlook? Thoughts about the possibility of life after death? Your beliefs?"

Sol became aware that he was involuntarily tapping his foot up and down, like a crystal meth addict. "I, uh, I'm trying to sort things out. I'm trying to, uh, you know..."

"Sort out what things?"

"I, uh, I really don't know. I, ah," he looked over at Norm, and Norm shot him a look that meant, *Don't blow it.* "You've got to excuse me, I'm really getting a migraine. The doctor said I could expect those. I'm sorry for wasting your time, but, ah, I really think I, ah, oughtta lay down."

Norm stepped in toward them both, smiling his LA talent-agent smile, and speaking confidentially to Cat. "If he just takes a break for five minutes, then I'm sure—"

"No," said Sol. "The interview's over. I'm sorry."

Cat looked at Norm in total disgust, as though he *had* to be kidding. "Oh, that's all right. I've just wasted an entire morning and blown a chance to interview Keith Richards because I was promised an exclusive from 'The *Great* Doctor Sol Harkens.' Thanks, Norm," she hissed. Then, in an almost Clint Eastwood rasp, "I'll be sure to remember it."

The *click click click* of her Christian Louboutins filled the room as she walked across Sol's hardwood floors and out the door.

"Well, you sure nailed that one," Norm said, opening a jar of martini olives from the bar and popping one into his mouth.

"Norm, back off, okay? You don't know what I'm going through," Sol said, pacing back and forth, feeling more like a caged animal every second, ready to go rogue.

"I don't know what you're going through?" said Norm, shooting a cuff, old-school, like Frank Sinatra or Johnny Carson. "You don't know what *I'm* going through! How do I book a gig for a guy whose main message is, 'I don't know'? Huh? Huh? Because people aren't gonna pay a hundred bucks a pop to hear a guy say, 'I don't know.'"

Sol said nothing, just clenched and unclenched his fists as he felt the panic rising.

"You're blowing it, pally," Norm told him, popping another olive into his mouth. "A whole career. I've seen it happen, and it's not pretty." He took one more olive for the road and headed for the door, where he stopped and faced Sol. "I'll see you around, Sol." And with that, Norm walked out and closed the door.

CHAPTER 13

I don't know, Sol Harkens thought to himself as he walked, half-drunk, partly stoned, and mostly smashed on his usual cocktail of sedatives and potato mash, otherwise known as vodka. He said the words over again, in his mind. *I DON'T know. I don't KNOW. I don't know...*

It was more confession than revelation, a cold and broken epiphany of a man who had *always* known.

Known everything.

Not just facts.

Especially not facts.

But known, without doubt, his own convictions.

Professors had called him "unusually focused."

Ah, but that was all just nonsense, folderol, and ballyhoo, he thought, *then and now.* He was not more or less focused. Indeed, he thought, he was more intensely focused when bleary-eyed on drink or drug. It was not a question of focus, it was simply a question of knowing.

Knowing who he was.

What he felt.

Knowing that for which he would live, die, kill, or sacrifice, if need be, his own life.

There was simply never a question.

Contemporaries plugged their ears with little buds through which they listened to would-be drug dealers shouting out invective and rage, and this they channeled through their own systems to reach greater heights, push heavier weights, run longer distances, or endure more pain.

Sol Harkens, on the other hand, had the recordings of Winston Churchill's wartime speeches in the summer of 1940, when all of Europe had fallen to Hitler's might and before America had entered the war, when the only thing between civilization itself and Hitler's "Narrrrzii's," as Churchill pronounced it in a long, guttural growl, was the rhetoric of a fat, bald, cigar-smoking alcoholic whose own cabinet was plotting his demise. It was then, in the words of Edward R. Murrow, that Churchill marshaled the English language, as no one but Shakespeare had done before him, and sent it out to do battle.

Unlike every hairsprayed politician of Sol Harkens's day, Churchill never had a speechwriter. There were no spin doctors. More than that, he was one of the few who knew that he had nothing at all capable of defeating the Nazi onslaught he fully expected would be unleashed against the island kingdom of Great Britain within a matter of weeks.

All of Europe had fallen to the Nazi blitzkrieg in barely less than a month, and days before Churchill delivered one of the most famous speeches in human history, France had surrendered to Hitler.

Churchill and England both stood utterly and completely alone.

The prime minister delivered his speech first before Parliament, which had received it with a shrug of the shoulders. Churchill was, in the words of one of his detractors, "a second-rate rhetorician." After the speech was delivered, someone suggested that he do it a second time, that evening, over the radio.

Churchill resisted.

He did not trust the wireless.

He was a man of sixty-five, overweight, a habitual smoker, and a drunk. And against the array of Hitler's seemingly invincible Panzer divisions and Göring's Luftwaffe, Churchill himself had nothing, he knew, but words.

And ultimately, the people of Britain and, indeed, all of occupied Europe, who sat beside clandestine radios and crystal sets straining to hear the words of the last democracy in Europe, had nothing but Churchill. Hope was gone. A darkness, not seen since the Middle Ages, had descended upon the continent.

Against his better judgement, more than likely somewhat the worse for drink, and smoking his cigar throughout his speech, Churchill gave the people of Britain, of occupied Europe, and of the as-yet uncommitted New World something more than hope. He gave them what he *knew*.

"What General Weygand called 'The Battle of France' is over," he growled, pulling not even the slightest of punches. He told his people, "I expect the battle of Britain is about to begin. Upon this battle depends the survival of Christian civilization. Upon it depends our own British life, and the long continuity of our institutions and our empire." He took a long drag on his cigar, exhaled the smoke, and delivered the hard truth to his countrymen, to the free world, and to those enslaved, who were hanging on his every syllable. "The whole fury and might of the enemy must very soon be turned on us. Hitler knows he will have to break us in this island or lose the war."

That was the hard truth, and now he simply told them what he knew.

Not what he hoped for, but what he expected because of that knowledge.

"If we can stand up to him, all Europe may be free and the life of the world may move forward into broad, sunlit uplands. But if we fail, then the whole world, including the United States, including all that we have known and cared for, will sink into the abyss of a new Dark Age, made more sinister, and perhaps more protracted, by the lights of perverted science."

By now, in the growing darkness of twilight, Sol Harkens had crossed the Brooklyn Bridge and walked down to one of his favorite spots, from which he could look across the river into the tiny island kingdom of Manhattan, illuminating the nighttime sky with a thousand thousand pinpoints of light. Behind each one, there was an apartment full of life, tragedy, human frailty, raucous joy, mindless denial, and, here and there, even faith. He could not help but think, listening to Churchill's words, of the skyline made darker by the absence of two towers that had fallen into what might well be, he thought, the abyss of yet another new dark age.

He had never before been so lost, so adrift, so full of self-doubt, and, indeed, self-loathing. He no longer knew.

Watching the lights and imagining the faces illuminated and hidden by each, he remembered his wife's challenge. Would he consider a different source? A different source of knowledge, since his own had so grievously abandoned him after his encounter with a beauty and love and serenity he had never imagined could exist? Would he consider a different source?

And then looking at the lights of the Manhattan skyline, preserved by a generation that had embraced, without shame or doubt, that other source of knowledge and earned for themselves the title of Greatest Generation, he listened to the very words that had strengthened the resolve of another island kingdom and, indeed, the generations that followed them, filling them with a sense of awe and wonder at the courage of their forebearers.

With a vodka buzz as great as the brandy-induced one that the cigar-smoking Churchill must himself have felt that night more than seventy years before, he heard the words that marched out to do battle with tyranny and vanquished their own self-doubt, their own loss of knowing.

"Let us therefore brace ourselves to our duties, and so bear ourselves, that if the British Empire and its Commonwealth last for a thousand years, men will still say *this* was their finest hour."

It was a drunken reverie, listening to Churchill's wartime speeches, not a sunlit epiphany, nor a full-throated, heartfelt hallelujah that made Sol Harkens say, "Why not? What have I got to lose? I know nothing. Nothing except that I have two boys whose lives will forever be impacted by the example I set for them."

He had nothing but doubt that this would be his finest hour, but at least he had resolved that he would comport himself in such a fashion that his children would not be ashamed.

He was going to see Pastor Vinny.

The next day, Sol drove the Benz through the lush and winding country roads of Connecticut to a nondescript, white clapboard church. A handyman on a ladder was painting and patching the slat-board wall.

The twilight courage of Sol's drunken reverie and Churchill's wartime rhetoric had long since left him.

This was the real folderol and ballyhoo.

He was going to see Reverend Lovejoy from *The Simpsons*.

Somebody please, give me a break and say it ain't so, he thought to himself. But he was already out there, and he might as well get it over with.

He opened the driver's side door of the Benz and let it close behind him, with the reassuring sound of Germanic precision engineering, lowered his $450 shades, and crossed over to the handyman on the ladder.

"'Scuse me," Sol said. "Can you tell me where I can find Pastor Vinny's office?"

The handyman looked down at him and spoke in a thick Bensonhurst accent.

"Yeah, but ya won't find him there."

Sol lifted the shades onto the top of his head. "Do you know where I *can* find him?"

"He's up on a ladder," the handyman said in a Brooklyn growl. "Now he's comin' down from the ladder."

The handyman stepped off the ladder and turned to Sol, who now saw the cross glinting in the sunlight against the man's T-shirt.

"Hi, I'm Pastor Vinny. You must be Doctor Harkens. I recognized ya from the pictures in the paper."

"Katy had a lot of good things to say about you, Pastor..."

"Vinny."

"Pastor Vinny," Sol said, smiling at the incongruity of the Brooklyn wiseguy clergyman. "You're not exactly what I expected."

"Yeah? Well, old habits die hard. I used to be in construction. And waste management. Did your wife tell you what else I was before I was a pastor?" Vinny crossed over to the freshly painted steps leading up to the church door and sat down, patting the plank next to him. "It's all right, the paint's dry. Have a seat, Doc. So, did she tell ya what I used to do?"

Sol sat down next to Pastor Vinny. "Is it important?"

"I dunno, you tell me. I was a wiseguy."

"A wiseguy," Sol repeated.

"Mobbed up," Pastor Vinny said, as if talking to a child who had wandered into a conversation without any frame of reference.

Sol just looked at him as the realization that he wasn't joking came over him. "You were a…?"

"Almost a made guy, except they had the books closed that year. Actually, that's not what I was before I was a pastor. What I really was, was Prisoner Zero Four Two Six Nine Four Eight Seven, U.S. Penitentiary, Tucson, Arizona."

"You were in prison?!"

"Did I stutter? Or, aren't you wired for sound? Yeah, I was in prison. And you know the only book they let you have in solitary?"

"Probably wasn't one of mine."

"Not even close." Pastor Vinny pulled out a pocket Bible and held it out for Sol to see. He could see that several pages were dog-eared, the binding well worn and almost falling off. "I read it front to back a dozen times. See, I didn't come to Jesus in any moment of epiphany. Not like your wife, she's got a real gift of faith. But I'm a street guy. So, ya know what stood out to me?"

"I honestly haven't a clue," responded Sol. "But this is one of the more interesting conversations I've had with a clergyman, so, please."

"What happened to the body?"

"You may have lost me."

Pastor Vinny sighed and tried another tack with the professor. "Jesus gets whacked, right?"

"I've never heard it put exactly that way."

"Well, now ya have," Pastor Vinny said, cutting Sol off, rhetorically. "What happens next? They stick His body in a tomb locked up tighter than a steel drum. An' then what happens? Ba-da-bing, it disappears."

Sol just looked at him. He had debated hundreds of clergymen, but he had never walked down this particular road before.

"Don't look at me like that. The body disappears, okay? Now, the Romans know they got a problem on their hands. 'Cause, if Jesus is resurrected, gone up to Heaven, then that's a miracle, an' that's not a little miracle; that's a big miracle! That's gonna turn a lotta people into believers. So the Romans gotta fine that body! An' the Romans were Italians! I know somethin' about that! They fried guys, they skinned 'em alive, they crucified 'em. But nobody ratted out where the body was. T'ink about that. Now, I had one a the toughest crews in New York, and I guarantee you any one a my guys woulda given up the body if they faced one tent' of what the disciples faced. But nobody broke rank. You know why? Huh? Hey, I'm talkin' to ya!"

Sol just stared at Pastor Vinny, mesmerized. It was like listening to a sermon delivered by Fat Clemenza from *The Godfather*.

"Nobody gave up the body because Christ was resurrected, that's why. That's what happened to da body. So, I said to myself, 'If the body really got resurrected, I better cut a deal wit' that guy.'" He paused and looked deep into Sol's eyes, and it occurred to Sol that Pastor Vinny knew.

Pastor Vinny leaned in toward him with a kind of brotherly compassion he had rarely felt from a stranger. "You know what it is to lose a child. But God's love for mankind was so perfect, an' His Son's love was so perfect, that He gave His only begotten Son so that the rest of us might find Salvation. Lemme ax you somethin'. When your soul lef' this world, wha'd it see?"

"My son."

"An' how'd he look?"

"So beautiful. So at peace."

"An' how did you feel?"

It was one of the most honest conversations Sol had ever had in his life. "I've never felt such love. Never." The memory washed over him and the peace of that love filled him again.

"That's because both of ya were bathed in the light an' the love of our Lord and Savior. You come to me and you say, 'Pastor Vinny. What's "let there be light" mean?' Your wife told me all about it. You say, 'I can't figure it out, I'm buyin' Wipe-Wowies, I'm buyin' mops, I'm goin' *oobatz*, here.' You wit' me?"

"You're on a roll," said Sol. "So, what's it mean?"

"Jesus was the Light of the World. It was the sense of His love that you felt. That was the serenity. What's Christmas? Huh? Huh? Don't just sit there, what's Christmas?"

It was a question no one had ever asked Sol before. He stuttered. "Uh...a holiday?"

"An' you're the one they call brilliant? *Marron*. It's Jesus's birthday, the day he was born. An' it falls at the darkest time of the year—because Jesus came to bring the world light. Look at what's goin' on in the world today. There's a darkness that's spreadin' across the globe. People gettin' whacked like they was in the middle ages, gettin' they heads cut off, burned alive. You don't t'ink evil's a real force? Trust me, Doc. I seen it. It's real."

Suddenly, Sol was thinking of Churchill's speeches, of the darkness that had once before threatened to engulf the world.

"Look at what those ISIS guys wear," said Pastor Vinny. "Their flag's black, their clothes are black. They're a cult of death. What did the SS wear? Black uniforms, skulls that glorified death. It's no different. An' whadda they got to offer? Just like the Nazis. Hatred. Murder. But Jesus spoke about lovin' our enemies. The answer to darkness is light. Jesus preached the antidote to hatred: love." Pastor Vinny put his arm around Sol, and Sol felt it was the gesture of a brother. "The Light o' the World wants ya to spread His message of love."

It was like being hit with a bucket of cold water. "Are you saying He *chose* me?" Sol asked, his bewilderment clear.

"Who better to choose than the biggest atheist of all? He literally let you see the light, an' now he's axin' you to spread it. An' just like God sent his only begotten Son to Earth with a message of love, He sent you your son." Pastor Vinny let that one sink in. "T'ink about that. He sent you your boy, Davey. That's how much He loves you."

"Oh, my God..." Sol said, and suddenly he knew. "Oh my God...oh my God..."

Pastor Vinny held him as close as he would a younger brother. "He *is* your God, Sol. And he's holdin' out his hand to ya. All you've gotta do now is take it."

CHAPTER 14

There was a stream that wound its way down from the hill above the white clapboard church in the Connecticut countryside. It ran clear, over rock and stone, dipping into shallows and bubbling up again as the landscape rose and fell, and wound itself like a mother's arms around the church.

It dipped beneath an old wooden bridge, and its sound was like a constant hum; not strong enough to splash, nor shatter itself against the rocks. It was a slow, flowing, still, small voice that ran clear above a sandy bottom. It opened out into a kind of pool and then narrowed again, and at that nexus, it gained strength, flowed stronger, like a rapid. This rush of water washed the granite rocks smooth in its oasis-like home in the green Connecticut foothills.

It was there that Sol Harkens, hitherto the most famous atheist in the English-speaking world, would be baptized.

At first, the notion of it seemed absurd to him. Epiphany is one thing. Fun's fun, but baptism? To Sol's Upper West Side sensibilities, the very sound of it conjured up, well...Baptists! Inbred hicks who married, if not their sisters, then at least their cousins, and clung, in the parlance of our times, with bitterness, in the face of a multiculturally changing world, to their guns and Bibles. Baptists! On the other hand, Sol was hip! Sol was cool! Sol was everything that made New York

New York! And Baptists were the antithesis of all that, of everything that made Sol *Sol*. Hosannah's and amens and abstinence? *Abstinence?!* Sol Harkens was the poster boy for indulgence! Everything worth doing, he constantly assured himself, was worth doing in excess! Sol was, in his own words, the head cheerleader for sex, drugs, and rock 'n roll!

And now, he was actually considering becoming baptized?!

"You've had an epiphany," Pastor Vinny said. "More den dat, you literally have seen da light. You wanna just walk away from dat, Doc?"

Sol sat on the church steps in silence. He had no idea what he wanted. He just kept involuntarily repeating, "My God. My God. My God..." The irony of those words was not lost on him.

Talking to Vinny, the former mobbed-up wiseguy, he suddenly realized what he had, indeed, experienced. He had seen his son! There was no question about it, he *knew* that. And he and his son were bathed in a light for which there was only one word: love. The purest form of love he could ever imagine existing, and which he had experienced this one and only time in his entire life. And if the experience was real, which he knew it was, if this all-encompassing light of love was real, which he knew it was, it had to have a source.

As hard as he fought against it intellectually, he knew that Pastor Vinny's words, uttered in their unmistakable Brooklyn accent, were not just intellectually true, but emotionally and, *God help me*, Sol thought—not again, without a sense of self-irony—spiritually true. He had felt that light of pure love, "Because both of y'uz were bathed in da light an' da love of our Lord and Savior."

There was no other explanation.

That loving light had to have a source.

And the source was God.

"You experienced exactly what the Aaronic Blessing talks about."

"I'm not, uh, familiar with the phrase."

"It's one a the most ancient blessings in the Judeo-Christian belief. It dates back thousands of years, before Jesus, when the Jews were in the desert wit Moses, an' Aaron was the high priest."

"I still don't know…I mean, I *should*, but—"

"Just listen to the words," the wiseguy priest told him. "An' then you'll know."

"What do you mean, 'know'?" asked Sol.

"Sol," Vinny said, seeing straight through Sol's con. "You know exactly what I mean. You didn't come out here to see me because you were a believer. You came out here because, for the first time in ya whole life, you didn't know nothin'. Not who you were, not what you believed, not what you experienced—not anythin' that made you *you*. You went t'rough somethin' that whacked you in the kneecaps, so you couldn't even stand on ya own two feet anymore. You came here because you didn't know, Sol."

"What are you, some kind of mind reader?" Sol asked.

"No, I'm a believer. But I never experienced what you did. You literally saw the light. Just listen to these words. Let 'em wash over ya, like that water in that stream over there washes over those rocks. This is the most profound blessing I t'ink there is in the whole Bible and you, more than anybody else in the whole world, *know* what it means."

Pastor Vinny laid his hands upon Sol's head like a father blessing his child. "May the Lord bless ya and keep ya," he said. "May the Lord light up his face to shine upon ya and be gracious unto ya. May da Lord turn his face toward ya an' grant ya peace."

"My God. My God..." Sol repeated again, not even realizing he was saying it. "That's exactly what happened."

"An' what did you feel?" Pastor Vinny asked. "For the first time in ya life?"

"Perfect love and...and..." Sol looked up, and suddenly realized the word he was looking for. "And peace."

"You know I went to seminary, right? I mean, I'm not just some storefront bum that said, 'Hallelujah, I'm a preacher!' I told ya, I never had a gift of faith like ya wife. An' God never granted me an epiphany like he did to ya. I actually studied this stuff like a street guy. I spent t'ree years in the hole, went t'rough the Bible an' went, "I gotta know what this was in the original!" So, I looked up words to see what dey meant, Aramaic an' Greek words. You know what 'peace' is in Hebrew?"

"Yeah, sure," said Sol. "It's the one Hebrew word almost everybody knows. It's *shalom.*"

"So whaddaya want, a gold star? You know what the root word is?"

"Don't have a clue," Sol said.

"The root word for *shalom,*" explained the wiseguy preacher, "is *shalem.* You know what that means?"

"No," said Sol.

"Of course ya don't! Because you never studied it! Because you never needed to you were an atheist! But all of a sudden, you *do* need to know, because you're here, and you need to know what that light was, and what it did to you. *Shalem* means 'whole.' Dat light of God's love made you whole for the first time in ya life. An' that gave you peace. An' now you know."

"Yeah," said Sol. He was fighting back tears. "I do. Now I know."

"You're a smart guy, Doc," said Pastor Vinny. "Go home. Fire up the ol' computer an' Google what baptism is an' who John the Baptist was. Look that one up, an' see what that does for ya. An' then, come back an' tell me what you wanna do about the fact that now you know. 'Cause there's really only t'ree t'ings you can do. Run from it, close your eyes to it, or accept it. Embrace it, an' live in that knowledge instead a hidin' from it."

Sol hugged Pastor Vinny like a brother and thanked him. He got back into his Benz and drove along the country road that wound its way along with the stream that washed down from the foothills, embracing the clapboard church, until, finally, he lost sight of it, drove aimlessly, and found himself in the long tunnel leading into Manhattan as the light of the setting sun blinded him.

When he finally got home, he did not open a bottle of vodka, as was his wont. He felt no need to pop a Xanax or a few diazepam. He just sat there, in the stillness, remembering the light.

Remembering Pastor Vinny's advice, he opened up his MacBook Air, turned it on, and Googled, "Who was John the Baptist?"

What popped up was, at first, an explanation that made him smile. The guy sounded like a dope-smoking, maggot-infested, hippie freak. He wore camel skin, had twigs in his hair, and lived in the Judean desert on a diet of locusts and wild honey. And his message was as simple as could be. He was not the Messiah, nor did he claim to be. He simply came to clear the way, and the way in which he did that was one of the oldest rituals of purification: to baptize.

To cleanse.

To return a person to the primordial, amniotic fluid of the earth and come out of it reborn in the light of the Lord. *John*

1:4-8: "In him was life; and the life was the light of men. And the light shineth in darkness; and the darkness comprehended it not. There was a man sent from God, whose name was John. The same came for a witness, to bear witness of the Light, that all men through him might believe. He was not that Light, but was sent to bear witness of that Light."

Sol read the last part again and said the words aloud. "He was not that Light, but was sent to bear witness of that light.

"My God." The words slipped involuntarily from his lips again, and he *knew.*

There were no guests, other than Sol's...*family*, he thought to himself, looking at his ex-wife and his children, whom he had sometimes thought of as nothing more than alimony and child-support payments that kept him in a Benz, rather than the Lamborghini he could otherwise have had. They were the children who he loved more than life itself, who were the fruit of a love he once shared with the woman whose touch he had once thrilled to.

They were gathered around the place where the stream widened out in a shallow pool, in the lush green countryside in front of the clapboard church.

Sol stood with Pastor Vinny, waist-deep in the pool of cool, running water that ran slowly past them, not rushing, but in a kind of stillness that was not still, but moved slowly, inexorably, to its own rhythm. He remembered the quote of Heraclitus. *Everything changes and nothing stands still. Everything flows and nothing stays. Everything flows and nothing abides. Everything gives way and nothing stays fixed. You cannot step twice into the same river.*

After today, everything would change for Sol Harkens. And that, too, he *knew*.

"Baptism," said Pastor Vinny, "is a public proclamation of our faith, for all to see, so nobody can cop out later and say it never happened. Sol, do you accept dat you are a sinner?"

"I do," said Sol, and he *knew*.

"Sol," said Pastor Vinny, "do you accept da Lord Jesus Christ as your Lord and Savior?"

"Yes," replied Sol, and he *knew*.

"I'm gonna depart from da normal baptism, an' ax ya somet'in'. What's ya name?"

Sol just looked at him.

"Don' just *look* at me," Pastor Vinny said. "Dis isn't what ya call a hard question. Pretend I'm a cop. What's ya name?"

"Sol?" said Sol tentatively.

"Good start," said Pastor Vinny. "An' dat is short for?"

"Solomon."

"Yo! Da man's a genius! An' do ya know what Solomon is, in da original Hebrew?"

"Uh..."

"By 'uh,'" said Pastor Vinny, "I take it ya don't. I do, 'cause I studied, an' you didn't. Solomon is from da Hebrew, *Schlomo*. You know what dat means?"

Sol just looked at him again.

"I'm axin' ya if ya know what ya own name means."

"No," said Sol.

Pastor Vinny lowered his voice to just above a whisper. "It means, 'His peace.' It's what God is about to give ya."

And with that, Pastor Vinny placed his hand at the back of Sol's head and the other at his waist, and laid Solomon Harkens back into the cool waters that washed over him in the same way they polished smooth the granite rocks of the riverbed, the stream in which Sol now found himself, and into which he could never step again.

"I baptize you," Pastor Vinny said, "in da name of da Father, da Son, an' of da Holy Spirit."

And when he pulled Sol back up out of the water, Sol *knew*, and he was smiling a smile that said he had found what he never knew he was looking for.

His peace.

He looked over at Katy. She was crying. The boys were teary-eyed as well. Sol came up out of the river and embraced them all.

He looked up at the sky above and the lush green of the earth all around. Calmly, he took a deep breath, as if it were his first, and let out a great sigh.

"You feel any different?" Gus asked.

"Yeah, Dad, you feel better, stronger, smarter, faster?" asked Connor.

Sol grabbed Connor playfully around the neck to noogie him. "Fast enough to catch you!"

Connor squealed with delight and ducked out of his father's grasp, as Sol chased him up the hill toward the church.

Katy looked at the two with a kind of longing. This was what she had always dreamt of. And yet, the dream was of her husband, not her ex-husband.

Gus, wise beyond his years, saw the emotions flashing across her face, looked at his mother, and said, "Careful, Mom. One day at a time."

Later that day, in what was no longer their house but what Sol had thought of for years as Katy's house, they sat out in the backyard as a family for the first time in years, finishing lunch.

Katy began to clear the table, taking the dishes back into the kitchen.

Connor tried out a few skateboard moves in the driveway, leaving Gus and Sol by themselves.

"Dad, what's it like to have a transformation like what you just did? I mean, how do you know it's real?"

"Because I *know*," Sol answered.

"How do you know it was God's love and not just your imagination?" Gus asked.

"Because it was the purest and most potent feeling. More real and brighter than the sun. It was a light of pure love."

"That's what you think now," Gus said, like a teenage prosecutor. "What if it's just a phase?"

"Now you sound like my father."

"Well," said Gus, "somebody's gotta be the adult around here. You don't have a very good record of that, do you, Dad?"

"No, I guess I don't."

"I mean, you and Mom made vows, and then broke them."

"You really go for the jugular, don't you, kid?"

Gus looked Sol in the eyes with his version of the thousand-yard stare. "I don't want Mom getting hurt."

Sol looked at him for a long time. "You know, I'm trying to figure out if you're the most decent kid I've ever met or an insufferable little—"

"Probably a little bit of both," Gus said.

Sol took a deep breath, then called out to Connor. "Connor, come here for a second, would ya?"

Connor skated over on his board, did an ollie, and then caught the board. "What's up?"

Katy rejoined the family at the table.

Sol looked up at her and the boys. "I owe all of you an apology," he said.

"Sol, you don't have to—"

"Yes, I do," Sol said. "For a long time, I made fun of all of you guys' faith. I couldn't understand it. And I didn't even want to try and understand it. I was all wrapped up in my own ego. But you never gave up on me, Katy. And for that, I'm eternally grateful."

Tears welled up in Katy's eyes, though she did her best to hide them. She kissed Sol gently on the forehead. Then, in spite of herself, she wiped away a tear and took his hand. This was the moment she had waited for, for so long.

Sol turned to Gus and Connor. "I told you guys," said Sol, "that I saw your brother. And that he said, 'Let there be light.'"

"Why?" asked Connor. "Was it dark?"

"No, doofus!" said Gus. "Jesus was the Light of the World. It means that Dad is supposed to spread the light of Jesus."

"Dad?! Our Dad?!"

"Yeah," said Sol. "Pretty weird, huh?"

They were all silent for a bit, each of them lost in their own thoughts.

And then Connor spoke up. "You know, when you think of it, Dad, Davey saved your soul."

The silence returned, and with it, each of them went into the most profound place of the human heart. It was as if, somehow, they were now, because they were family, connected to Sol's vision. As if they could see Davey holding out his arms, could literally see the light, could *feel* Davey's embrace, the softness of his skin, the warmth of his eyes...Could hear him whisper into each of their hearts, "Daddy, let there be light."

And Sol *knew* it was true.

They all did.

And in that knowledge, for the first time in what seemed like an eternity of time, they were a family once again.

CHAPTER 15

It was difficult for Sol to drive home that evening because, for the first time in a long time, the tricked-out loft in the hippest section of the Village, the shrine to his ego, the lair for endless dreams of Russian supermodels and impressionable grad students, the perfect bachelor's pad, the place he had clung to, at times fearing to leave it for weeks on end like a PTSD victim, the scene of subconscious, predawn buys of carnival-hawked cookware, was no longer his home.

The place he had just left, the house in Connecticut where his children and his ex-wife lived, the place where, for all his short eight years on the planet, Sol had kissed his son Davey good night—that place receding in the rearview mirror—*that* was home.

It was certainly what he had once meant to be his home. He could remember every detail of the first time he saw it, just over sixteen years ago. Could it have been that long? Katy was pregnant with their firstborn, their sweet Davey, and he had just settled the court case with Maurice Guibert, and the judge had awarded him more money in one afternoon than his own father had made during an entire lifetime.

In one afternoon, he had gone from being an associate pro-fessor of English literature at Columbia University, living in faculty housing on 113th off of Lex in Harlem, just as it was about to become hip, with Bill Clinton moving in, to a semi-well-to-do, soon-to-be father in need not of a three-story walk-up with a New York galley kitchen and junkies on the subways, but a home, a real one, with a yard where they could lie out on blankets, sip lemonade and eat watermelon, and watch their baby grow, and later, where he could hang a basketball hoop up on a garage door. It amazed him how quickly he had gone from being the hippest professor on campus to a man who felt his wife's swollen belly and knew that the kick coming from within was his son, his soon-to-be-born boy. And that now—more than anything else in the world, more than writer or lecturer, or hottest professor on campus, as he prided himself on the fact that he was—to daddy.

Far from fearing it, he was shocked at how much he longed for it. He felt like breaking out into a rousing version of "My Boy Bill." He was, indeed, every cliché imaginable. He wanted to create, in his own image, the family he had never had as a child. He was an army brat. They had moved nine times in twelve years when he was growing up. He wore his athletic and intellectual prowess like armor. If he didn't stick around long enough to make any real friends, he was determined that it would be long enough to make an impression. He'd be an adolescent Lone Ranger—"Who was that masked man?"—except that he had no faithful companion named Tonto. Indeed, if someone were to ask him, "Who was your best friend growing up?" he would have been at a loss to name one. Books were his best friends. Ideas. Other kids were, well, not someone you wanted to become close to, because he knew that, sooner rather than later, he would be leaving them behind.

As an army brat, he almost had the attitude of a World War Two veteran. Don't get close to the new guys, they'll be dead soon enough.

The way you combat being an outsider is by positioning yourself as superior to all those that are inside. It's not that you're not part of *their* circle; they're not part of *yours*. He used to love to watch William F. Buckley, a pretty geeky thing for a twelve-year-old to do, but when you move around a lot, television is a constant. His fascination with Buckley had nothing to do with the latter's political views. Truth be told, he couldn't care less one way or the other. What fascinated him was the man's mastery.

It was the same attraction that everyone his age felt for Muhammad Ali.

You couldn't touch him.

Float like a butterfly, sting like a bee.

That was Sol Harkens, the intellectual hybrid of Bill Buckley and Ali. Untouchable because he was superior, superior because he was alone. And lonely was something he would never admit to anyone.

And now, suddenly, the boy who had moved almost every other year of his life had a chance at the home he'd never known, the money to buy it, the wife to fill it with love, and the child to whom he could be the father he'd always longed for, instead of the embittered, alcoholic Vietnam vet whose love he'd yearned for and whose presence he'd feared.

When Katy said, "I don't want to raise our child in this city," and suddenly, there was the money to buy their dream house in the country, he'd felt, for an atheist, the most blessed of all men.

He *wanted* to mow the lawn.

He *wanted* the white picket fence.

He *wanted* barbecues and touch football games with his kids, wanted to toss them in the air and split the silence in which he had grown up with their laughter.

He wanted to be Ward Cleaver.

They wanted a place where the air was clean, where the sidewalks didn't smell of urine of the homeless, a place where flowers bloomed, where there were trees that changed colors with the seasons, streams, farmers markets, and neighbors you could wave to. He wanted the miracle of a boring evening at home.

But no place they looked at seemed to have it, that indefinable quality that said, *We can be happy here.*

And then they walked into the place on Meadowview Court, and even the name of it was right, because the backs of all the houses looked out beyond their wooden fenced-in yards to a beautiful meadow, in which Bambi would have felt right at home.

Sol was physically a big man, and the house had the comforting feeling of bigness to it, while seeming cozy, as well. The entrance had double doors, and as soon as one entered, it was as if one saw the whole house at once. The foyer fed straight into a family room, and there were no walls between that and the step-down great room with floor-to-ceiling glass and high ceilings that looked out into what seemed to Sol to be the most perfect backyard on Earth. There was a tree that had been hit by lightning that had almost toppled over, almost died, and yet there was a resilience in it, a strength, and it continued to grow, albeit at an angle. It was the perfect tree for climbing for his boys when they were small. They could clamber up the roots that had almost been torn away from the earth but continued to grow and became even stronger, then walk up the trunk that angled off over the sloping yard.

He put in a tire hanging from a rope that they could use as a swing, in which he could twirl them around as they laughed with delight. There were morning glories that grew up the side of the tree, and off the great room was a sunroom where, even on the dreariest day of winter, there was a happy kind of light.

A basketball hoop was nailed up above the garage door, and the backyard itself sloped down toward the meadow beyond their fence. When the boys had their first plastic trikes and cars, he pushed them down the hill. They would have races and elaborate pirate games, and the tree that leaned at a forty-five-degree angle would become their pirate ship. They had swordfights and water-gun fights, and on the Fourth of July, there were old-fashioned fireworks on the meadow, which dipped down to a small-town, open-air amphitheater, a little stage on which local bands would play in time to the fireworks. It was, in short, a village green, complete with bandstand, draped with patriotic bunting, and they simply opened up the gate on their backyard, took out a blanket and lawn chairs, and watched the small-town fireworks with the smells of hot dogs and hamburgers filling the air.

It was, quite simply, paradise.

And even though his wife was a devout Christian and Sol was earning a good living being a professional atheist, it was almost never a cause of friction. Not in the beginning, at least. His attitude toward his wife's religion was amusement, more than hostility—up until the day that his boy Davey's eyes rolled back into his head and he fell back onto the ground, twitching as if jolted by an electric current, the tiny muscles in his arms and legs spasming and a strange, guttural sound coming from his throat as he went into a full grand mal seizure. And then, their world became the cancer ward.

The diagnosis was a glioblastoma multiforme, a tumor pressing against his brain and so virulent that the doctor said it didn't matter whether they got the tumor out or not. In terms of excising the malignancy, the surgery had been a complete success. The problem, the doctor explained, was they could remove Davey's entire brain and the tumor would still grow back on the brain stem.

The tumor always won.

It always came back.

It always vanquished.

It was never cured.

And the greater the toll the tumor began to take on Davey's tiny body, the more fervently Katy prayed, and the more Sol's hatred for those prayers grew along with them.

She was praying to the God who, if he existed at all, was a child molester.

And she had the nerve to pray that *his* soul be redeemed by the deity to whom she paid worship. He was enough a student of ancient history to know that, in the ancient sect of Moloch, parents offered up their own children in sacrifice to the supposed god.

Well, not Sol.

Never Sol.

With the death of their child came the death of their marriage, and the home that he had so longed for and had loved so well became a prison from which he was only too glad to escape.

Instead of a dad, he was a weekend dad.

And it broke his heart.

He wanted to tuck his boys in at night. He missed the family they once had been, but he retreated into his own childhood and adolescent armor. If he could not have that for which he longed, he would have disdain for it instead.

His career as a professional atheist grew with the vehemence of his hatred of all that he felt had robbed him of his child, of this Christian cult, as primitive as any that boasted fire-breathing idols into whose flames ancients sacrificed their dearest children.

And then he had had the car crash.

And then he had seen his son.

And then he had seen the light and felt a greater love than he had ever known. Now his life was whiplashed, back out of the armor of smugness and superiority, into the man who missed so much—his family, his home, his wife.

A few days after his baptism, Sol received a call from his old college roommate, Chuck. The man he'd bunked with and with whom he'd frequently partied in college had become a very successful stockbroker, had become a millionaire actually. The only price for it was that he had never been home.

Chuck was a father in name only, and now, at fifty-four years of age, he had been diagnosed with pancreatic cancer and had no more than six months to live. He called Sol up and asked him a question that was so heartbreakingly sad, it took all of Sol's strength not to allow his voice to break.

"When your kids were little," Chuck asked, "where did you take them on vacations?"

"What do you mean?" Sol answered.

"I mean, well," Chuck said, "I'm not going into the office anymore now that I've been diagnosed, and I want to take the kids on a trip, and I don't know where to take them. I never went on a vacation with them. My wife always went into the country with them for the summer, but...you know, we've been divorced for ten years. I mean...where do you take them?"

It was, perhaps, the saddest question anyone had ever asked Sol.

"You can't ever go wrong with the beach," Sol answered. "You know, up to the Cape? There's a ton of stuff to do there. Do they like the beach?"

"Yeah," Chuck said hesitantly. "I guess. Sure."

Sol gave him the name of a few inns in which he had stayed when the children were younger. He said he didn't know if they were open any longer. It had been over eight years since Davey had died, over eight years since *he* had taken his kids on a summer vacation. And now, his friend was out of time.

Sol determined that *would not* happen to him. He had not only found Christ, he had found his family once again.

Sol was in a mode of making up for lost time. Before his baptism, Sol had, of course, started studying the Bible—the New Testament, to be exact. He devoured the text, trying to decipher the message he had spent a majority of his life denying. He was surprised by how easy it was to read and reread, how clear it was, and yet how much thought and study it demanded.

Shortly after recommitting himself to his family, Sol was again tempted by the glitz and glamor the camera and fame offered. Norm, never one to let go of a prize catch, had secured him a second interview with Cat Ryerson after the first one ended disastrously.

Sol listened to the voicemail from Norm and considered his options.

Sol recognized he was a new man, reborn, and yet, he understood his life would be completely destroyed if the truth about him got out. It was a betrayal of everything he had stood for. His fans would decidedly turn against him, wouldn't they? Book sales would plummet, as would his public stature. No more sold-out lecture halls or awards banquets. No more invitations to fancy soirees, no more posh Hamptons weekends with New York society. He would likely become a joke, a pariah, the object of scorn and ridicule.

Is that what rebirth meant? Annihilation of what was before? What was it that Jesus said? Something about denying yourself, taking up your cross, and following Him.

That certainly seemed unequivocal. But did Sol possess the courage?

If he turned down the interview, Ms. Ryerson might well write about his refusal instead, concocting myriad reasons for his uncharacteristic timidity. After all, Sol had never backed down from a debate. He typically sought out controversy and challenges, and so he wrestled with his reluctance to submit himself to scrutiny by his friends, the same people who had delivered his incredible fame over the years.

He realized that now was the least opportune moment to hide from the public. He needed to make a statement, to reassert himself.

Sol called Normie back and told him, "Sure. I think it's a great idea."

Norm thanked all the literary agent gods that his client had returned to what senses he had. He would now undo all the damage he had previously done with his first "I don't know" interview. He could ride the wave of atheistic glory once again and top the charts, ensuring Norm's livelihood for years to come.

Sol had assured Norm that the "I don't know" phase of his life was over, and poor Normie Zee thought that was a good thing. He envisioned having his vodka-guzzling, pill-popping star back in his pocket, lining it with every debate, appearance, and book release.

Cat Ryerson was to meet Sol at his apartment at six thirty the next evening.

"You feel up to this interview, pal?" Norm said, only slightly anxious.

"Absolutely," Sol reassured him with a confidence Norm had not seen in his client since before the accident.

"Great, great! Listen, pal, I might be a little late. I've got an early dinner meeting at Le Veau d'Or. But if you really feel good about this interview..."

"Hundred percent," said Sol. "Give my regards to Cathy. And have the veal, it's the best in the city."

"So, it's okay if I'm maybe fifteen, twenty minutes late, right, pal? I mean, you're back on track, right?"

"Couldn't be better," Sol told him.

"You look good. You're laying off the sauce and the pills, right?" Norm needed all the reassurance he could get.

"Haven't touched a drop."

"And the Percocet? The diazepam, the Xanax?"

"Flushed 'em down the toilet," Sol said.

"Well, there's no need to get crazy," Norm said. "You might need one!"

"Nah. Never felt better."

That should have been a warning sign to Normie Zee, but like a five-year-old that wants to believe that Santa is coming on Christmas morn, Norm just said, "Great! I'll just be fifteen, twenty minutes late."

He was all smiles when he walked into Sol's apartment in the middle of the interview, having tasted the well-reviewed veal and partaken in a few glasses of red wine, until he saw the smiling Sol sitting opposite the enraptured Cat Ryerson.

"And he said, 'Let there be light.' And when he said that, I felt the most perfect love I've ever felt in my life," Sol told Cat.

Norm's heart sank. He felt a wave of nausea wash over him. Betrayal did not feel like a strong enough word.

Cat was furiously scribbling every word in her notebook, a happy reporter who had just landed the most amazing scoop. "And you believe that love was?"

"God's love," Sol answered without a doubt.

"I can quote you on that?" Cat looked like she'd just caught a bird. "The author of *Aborting God*?"

"Has been saved by the love of Jesus Christ and the grace of a compassionate God. Yes," said Norm's client.

"Wow!" said Cat.

And even though he knew that he was losing his most valuable client, Norm couldn't help but think how much Cat sounded like Christopher Walken when she said, "Wow!"

"Waahh-hoooow," she said again. "So, what're you gonna do now? Are you going to, like, become a minister? Or a monk? Or—"

"I don't know. That's part of what I'm trying to sort through. What exactly is God's plan for me?"

"Waahh-hoooow!" she said again. "Wowie-wow-waahh-hooow! Okay. Waahh-hooow."

"What God's plan is for you?!" Norm interjected incredulously.

"Uh huh," Sol said, an idiotic, innocent grin on his face.

"Waahh-hooow! I mean...waahh-hooow! So, cool. I appreciate you giving me the exclusive. The biggest atheist in the world just had a come-to-Jesus moment. How do you think your fans are going to take this?"

"I don't know. I hope it opens them up to the possibilities of God's love."

"I wouldn't hold my breath," Norm said drily. He could practically see the dollar bills flying away from him.

"Then, why should your fans read your books?" Cat asked.

"They shouldn't."

"Waahh-hooow! Okay," responded Cat, still shell-shocked from the major revelation.

"You realize you've just thrown away your career," Norm confronted Sol, his eyes seeking out anything familiar in the man sitting on the couch, in the client he thought he had known so well.

Sol stared back. "And saved my soul."

"Waahh-hooow!" said Cat, Walkenesque still. "Okay! Thanks, guys. I've got a story to file and a deadline to meet."

"Help yourself to a Wipe-Wowie, if you'd like. Plenty more where they came from," Sol said, as her Louboutins click-click-clicked down the hall and out the door.

Norm went to the bar, where the vodka had been replaced with a bowl of honey-roasted peanuts. "Hm!" he said appreciatively. "I love these things!" He turned to Sol. "Well, pal. I hope Jesus can book you another gig, because I sure can't. As my client, you're fired."

"I kind of figured that's the way it would be, Norm, but at least we can still be friends."

Norm popped what was left of the peanuts in his hand into his mouth, brushed the crumbs from his palms, shot his cuffs old-school Sinatra-style, and straightened his pocket square. "Sol. I was never your friend. It was just business. You were an arrogant jerk, but you made me a lot of money. Now, you're an arrogant jerk who believes in Jesus. And whatever you're selling, I don't have a buyer for it. See ya 'round, pally."

Sol watched as Norm stormed toward the door. "Want a Wipe-Wowie?" he called out.

There was no answer, just the door closing behind his former agent.

And with that, the door closed on Sol's professional atheist career as well.

Strangely enough, he couldn't have cared less. Sol felt at peace with his decisions for the first time in a long time.

A knock at the door startled him from his reverie.

"Come on in," said Sol. "Did you change your mind about the Wipe-Wowie?"

To his surprise, Katy walked in, wearing a simple sweater and slacks and looking absolutely stunning, Sol thought.

"Oh," he said. "I thought you were my former agent."

"Former?"

"Norm just fired me."

"I'm sorry," she told him. And he knew she meant it. Her sincerity was something he'd always appreciated, even when it had rankled him after their divorce.

"I'm not," Sol replied. "Would you like a drink?"

Katy looked at him, almost in horror, as Sol crossed from the living room area into the kitchen.

"I've got raspberry iced tea, lemon iced tea, decaf lemon iced tea, passionfruit iced tea—"

"You're really into iced tea."

"They're actually pretty good. Want one?"

"No," she said. "But you go right on ahead."

He pulled a bottle of iced tea from the fridge, smacked the bottom of the bottle so that it made that satisfying, cap-releasing sound, twisted the cap off, and took a drink.

Katy pulled out her iPhone. "Sol, you know how you've been racking your brain about what 'Let there be light' means and what to do about it?"

"Yeah."

"Maybe it's just as simple as this." She hit the main light dimmer and turned off the lights in the apartment. At the same time, she turned on her phone's flashlight app.

"That's it?" said Sol.

"On the darkest night of the year," Katy said, "maybe it's just as simple as people all over the world turning on their flashlights, pointing them up at the heavens, and lighting up the darkness."

"Let there be light," Sol said.

"And we could have an app, where if people texted 'LTBL,' it would automatically make a donation to their local food bank."

This was like the old days with Katy, where she would start a sentence and he would finish it. Where they would feed off each other's intellect.

"And we could have a thing on the app where kids could go into a chat room. I'm thinking in places like Europe or the Middle East where kids can't ask about Christ, because they could get killed, but they can download an app, and if they have questions about Christ, they can ask kids their own age," Sol added.

"So we'd be nurturing people's bodies *and* their spirits," Katy concluded.

"Light into darkness," Sol said, and Katy nodded her head.

They stood there side by side, mulling the idea over and grinning ear to ear. Katy had found the Rosetta Stone to 'let there be light,' and now they were partners in making it come to reality. The silence was the silence of the high of great joy and the descent down to an earth still scorched here and there by the battles of their divorce, marred with the litter of bitter memories. Neither of them wanted to say good night, nor was there much to say about the newborn baby of "let there be light." It was like a garden hose when the pressure goes down to zero.

"Well, I should get going," Katy finally said.

"Yeah," said Sol. "I'll walk you out."

"Sol, it's twenty feet. It's not like I need an armed guard."

"Maybe I just want to walk you out," said Sol.

"You want to get rid of me 'cause you have someone else coming over?" Katy regretted the words the moment she had spoken them. "I'm sorry. I didn't mean that, it's just—"

"A well-deserved old habit," Sol said. "It's all right. I've definitely earned it. But no, I don't have anyone else coming over."

Katy flushed with embarrassment. "I mean, not that it's any of my business if you do—"

"Katy," Sol said, cutting her off.

"What?"

Sol bit his lip, knowing he was about to cross a certain Rubicon, not only of the mind but of his life. "Would you, I mean, could we...uh..."

"Could we what?" Katy asked.

"Could we go out to dinner sometime this week?" The words rushed from his mouth like that of a nervous schoolboy.

Katy looked at him, knitting her eyebrows as if to ask, *What's the big deal about that?* "Absolutely. I'm sure the boys would love to, especially if it's Chick-fil-A."

"No," said Sol, putting his hand against the door, in essence blocking any means of escape. "I don't mean you and me and the boys. I mean you and me."

"Out to dinner," said Katy.

"Yeah," said Sol, smiling what he hoped was his most charming smile.

"Like a date?" asked Katy.

"No," Sol said hurriedly. "Just, you know, a dinner. Just, you know, in the sense that we have to set a date for it, so in that sense, it's a date, it's a dinner date. But, you know, just calendar-wise."

"A calendar...date...dinner...date."

"Right," said Sol. "There's this new restaurant that just opened and, you know, it just opened, so that would be nice to try, and it's near the house, I mean, your house, and we could talk about the app—"

"Sure."

"Yeah?"

"Why not?" said Katy.

"Okay!" said Sol. "I accept."

"*You* accept?" said Katy. "*You* asked *me*!"

"And I accept your answer. Which was yes."

"I think we better quit while we're ahead."

"Good idea. Wednesday at eight?"

"Thursday at seven," Katy said.

"It's a date!" said Sol. "I mean, calendar-wise."

"Sol," said Katy, "you're blushing."

"Niacin rush. Vitamins."

And both of them smiled.

The awkwardness flooded back into the room again. They were standing at the door, about to say good night, that moment when couples usually kiss.

"I think I'd better go," Katy said, and Sol moved his hand from the door and opened it for her. She smiled. "This is really exciting. I mean, the app—"

"Absolutely," Sol said, and smiled back.

He watched as she walked down the hall to the elevator and pushed the button. Katy turned and smiled back at him, then heard the door and entered the elevator, still smiling as she pushed the button and the doors closed.

Sol stood there at his doorway a long while.

Smiling.

CHAPTER 16

The campus of NewComHiTech was adjacent to the Science, Technology and Advanced Research annex of the University of Delaware. This was the Silicon Valley of the East Coast.

Sol and Katy had already tried three other high-tech firms in the area and been turned down by each. The kind of app they were talking about was an expensive one, and though Sol had real estate holdings, most of his assets were not liquid. Plus, he was, technically, not only out of work with his speaking tour cancelled, but he was in breach of contract on his next two books, which were supposed to be atheist tomes similar to the ones he'd written throughout his entire career.

They had gotten an oblique reference to NewComHiTech from Jason Baker of JB Cyber Solutions. After he had heard what they wanted to do, he said, "Try Sally Darwan. This might be up her alley. You never know."

Sally Darwan turned out to be the founder and president of NewComHiTech, a very successful startup that specialized in constructing apps. They were located in the New Age Industrial Park adjacent to the Science, Technology and Advanced Research annex of the University of Delaware, and indeed, it looked more like an extension of the university than anything else. There were green areas with little fountains, nice lunch spots with wooden tables, high-rises that, while clean in their lines, tried not to be cold and impersonal. The whole place seemed to be infused with a Zuckerberg idea of a high-tech campus. Some geeks were on skateboards. Jeans and T-shirts and the occasional pair of Bermuda shorts seemed to be the uniform of the day. There was a studied informality to the place.

If geeks built Disneyland, it would look exactly like this.

Sol and Katy located building Five North, signed in at the front desk, received their security ID badges, had a security guard key card the elevator to grant them access to the inner sanctum on the upper floors of the high-rise, and looked at each other with a look that admitted not defeat, but the grim fact that this was their last shot.

They were shown into a glassed-in boardroom by the be-spectacled receptionist. Neither of them said anything; they just waited. Sol took out his iPhone and texted. Katy ran through her prepared notes, even though she knew the pitch by heart.

The door opened smoothly and in walked Sally Darwan, an attractive South Asian woman who appeared to be in her early forties. She was in a Donna Karan, dress-for-success mode. "Hello," she greeted them, offering her hand and speaking in a soft, South Asian accent. "I'm Sally Darwan." She placed the accent on the last vowel of her name. "And this is the head of our development, Ted Forrester."

"Pleasure to meet you," said Katy, shaking hands with Sally and the lanky, somewhat goofy-looking techno-geek, Ted Forrester. He had stringy blond hair that hung down, covering his eyes, and actually had a pocket protector in his left shirt pocket.

The boardroom was as sterile as a CIA interrogation room. Nothing on any surface top, nor any wall, betrayed the slightest hint of any conversations that had taken place here. There was one glass wall that separated the room from the corridor of offices, and another one opposite it, which afforded a view of the food court on the campus below.

"Thank you for agreeing to see us on such short notice," Katy said, getting ready to launch into the pitch.

"That's quite all right," said Sally. "Jason Baker is an old friend, and he spoke very highly of you both. He's actually read a number of your books, Doctor Harkens."

"Then," said Sol, "he has my deepest condolences."

Sally laughed charmingly, Katy smiled, and Ted wore that Steve Buscemi look of noncomprehension.

"What we've come to discuss—" said Katy.

Sally cut her off by raising her hand. "Jason told me everything about it. I don't want to be rude, but I'm a quick study, and I have a tight schedule today."

That's it. We're sunk, thought Sol.

"Well," said Katy, pulling out part of her presentation, determined to get in her pitch, when Sally cut her off again.

"I'm sure that your presentation is quite impressive, but why, exactly, have you come to see me with this? We are a high-tech company. We've never made a religious app before."

Sol leaned in toward her and decided to ditch their presentation and cut to the chase, the heart of the matter. "There's a very real darkness that's engulfing almost all of humanity right now. Cults of death cutting people's heads off. Millions of refugees. People living like slaves in North Korea. We think the antidote to that darkness is light. And the antidote to hatred—" he took a deep breath, "is the love of Jesus Christ."

Silicon Valley types had made up the core of his former audience. The mention of Jesus Christ, to most of them, was akin to someone loudly belching during the silence between movements of a symphony.

"So," said Sally, "how, exactly, will your project solve anything?"

That was Katy's opening. "By literally shining a light into darkness," she started.

"The app we'd like you to design," said Sol, "would tell people across the globe exactly when to turn on their cell phone flashlights and turn them skyward."

"What we envision," Katy continued, "is a band of light slowly encircling the earth, light taking the place of darkness."

She and Sol had a natural rhythm. It was seamless. Pitch after pitch, it had sharpened as they rediscovered their natural synchronicity.

"We want to cut a deal with NASA," said Sol, "and have a satellite photo of that band of light spreading around the world. Sort of a selfie for God."

"Cut a deal with NASA?" Ted volunteered. "You don't think that's a bit overly ambitious?"

"No," said Katy, completely ignoring Ted and fixing Sally with her eyes, woman to woman, and thinking, *there's something more there than just that.* So she pushed ahead with the pitch. "In addition, if people text the letters 'LTBL,' they'll automatically be making a donation to their local food bank. The point is, we want to feed people physically, as well as spiritually."

Sol jumped in before the techno-geek could fire another salvo. "We'll have people standing by in chat rooms, volunteers from churches all over the world, ready to engage anyone who has a question about the love of Jesus Christ." He stopped talking, and let that lie there. They were either going to buy into the idea or not.

"You want to proselytize," Sally said. It was a statement, not a question.

"Absolutely and without apology," said Katy, still looking straight into her eyes.

"We will proselytize life with as much vigor as ISIS proselytizes death," Sol added, coming in right on cue.

Sally looked over at Ted, then back to Sol and Katy. "Such a thing would be very controversial," she told them.

It was now Katy's turn to lean in toward her. "ISIS uses social media to promote violence and murder. Why should we be barred from using the exact same tools to promote life?"

"In the face of darkness," Sol said, "let there be light."

"In the face of hate," Katy said, picking up Sol's cadence, "let there be love."

That was pretty much it. That was the pitch. The rest would be just getting into the weeds of the how of it all. But the *what* of it all was lying there on the table between them.

"There's an old salesman's saying," Sol had told Katy. "Whoever speaks first loses. Once we've laid out the premise, we don't say a word. If there's water, we start drinking, and we don't stop until they speak."

"Agreed," Katy had said. And now, both of them reached for their little bottles of room-temperature imported water, broke the plastic seals, and began to drink.

There was not a sound in the room but that of their drinking.

Sally just smiled. This was not her first rodeo. "Whoever speaks first loses," she said. "Is that right? Or are both of you just suffering from spontaneous dehydration?"

"I haven't a clue as to what you are talking about," Sol said, smiling disingenuously.

"Mm," said Katy. "I'm just a housewife, so what do I know?"

Sally smiled back at them. For the first time, there was a chemistry in the room. "Are either of you aware of my background?" she asked.

"Your background?" Katy responded, with that "uh-oh" feeling rising up in her gut.

"I was born in Pakistan, and a Muslim."

To say that the silence that followed was an awkward one would have been an understatement.

"I was forced into a marriage," Sally continued, "when I was fourteen to a very brutal man. He used to beat me. And when I ran back to my father for protection, he beat me for disobedience to my husband. And when I said I would leave him, I was told I would be killed. An honor killing. But I was lucky. I was able to come here, to the United States. And here, I was saved, quite literally, by the love of Christ."

Now it was her turn to let that lie there on the table between them. Sol and Katy looked at each other in disbelief, then back at Sally.

"I don't believe that you are here by chance. I believe you were sent to me." Sally turned to the techno-geek. "Ted." And it wasn't the usual tone. It was the tone one would use with a well-trained pet, to give commands like "Come," "Sit," Stay," etc.

Ted brushed the stringy blond hair away from his eyes, and said, "It can be done, that's not a problem. It looks to me like we have roughly six months to get it up and running."

"Then I'll give you five, Ted," Sally said.

"I was counting on that," he said, smiling.

Sally rose to signify that the meeting was over. "Christmas Eve. When the Light of the World first shone."

She extended her hand to Sol and Katy. "You have a partner, Doctor and Mrs. Harkens."

Katy shook Sally's hand, and then said, somewhat embarrassedly, "Actually, we're not..."

"We were," Sol said, almost as awkward as a schoolboy. "But, we're not, now...Mr. and Mrs."

Sally smiled at them, with a smile that was at once ancient and warm. "Really? How very odd. You have the look of newlyweds."

Before they started their round of pitches, Sol had told Katy that another one of the rules of salesmanship was never to talk about what had just transpired in the office until you were well outside the building. One never knew with whom one was riding in an elevator.

And so, Sol and Katy rode down to the first floor, not talking, just grinning from ear to ear.

They said nothing as the elevator doors opened and they crossed the lobby back to the front desk. They handed in their security badges and thanked the guard, and then walked across the polished floor and out the glass doors of building Five North.

They waited until they had rounded the corner, out of sight of anyone exiting building Five North, and then they both burst at once.

"ALL RIGHT!" exclaimed Sol.

"WE DID IT!" Katy rejoiced.

They high-fived each other, grins spread wide as they met each other's eyes. And there was that awkward moment as they held each other's hands longer than a high-five requires.

The electricity was there, the same electricity that had passed between them almost twenty years before, when they had met, when Sol was just a teaching assistant and Katy a senior in English literature. There was an instant attraction between them, and though they were only a few years apart, Sol was faculty and Katy was a student. They were both determined that no impropriety would occur will Katy was under his tutelage. Sol had counted down the days to Katy's graduation. And while she was still wearing her cap and gown, he asked her out on their first date.

And there it was. The old electricity was back, as was the sense that, somehow, to act on it would have been improper.

They had come in separate cars, Katy from Connecticut and Sol from Manhattan.

"So," said Sol, awkward as a teenager.

"Yeah," said Katy.

"I guess," said Sol, "we ought to head back. We'll both hit traffic."

"Yeah," said Katy.

"Right," said Sol. "We're still on for Thursday, right?"

"Thursday?" said Katy, as if it were the first time she ever heard the word.

"Do not do that," said Sol. "We have a date—on the calendar—for dinner."

"Right," said Katy.

"Thank you, Jesus," said Sol.

"One doesn't take the Lord's name in vain," Katy said, smiling.

"Trust me," said Sol, "that was not in vain. That was heartfelt."

They both smiled again and walked toward the parking structure. And there was, once again, the awkwardness as Katy said, "My car's on five."

"Mine's on three," said Sol.

"Right."

"Right. So, I'll see you Thursday," Sol said.

"It's a date," Katy said.

And this time, neither of them mentioned the calendar.

Sol's apartment was now the headquarters of Operation: Let There Be Light. The dining room table was strewn with papers, boxes piled high in every corner, and four desktop computers where once there was only Sol's MacBook Air. In short, it was an organized mess whose organization was known only to a select few. But somehow, it functioned, and a tremendous amount of productive work took place there.

Almost all of Sol's former associates had deserted him. *Not unlike*, he thought, *rats streaming from the bilge of a sinking ship*. He had not realized how much he had grown to depend upon Norm and his staff, his publisher Sylvie and her staff, and the business manager of which he no longer had any need since he no longer had a business. Indeed, the only person who had stayed with him, and this at no cost, was his publicist Tracee. She was devoting as much of her energy to the project as Sol and Katy, and somehow managed to continue her work as a freelance publicist in the wee hours of the morning.

As Sol and Tracee worked putting out publicity kits about the Let There Be Light Christmas Event, the television set played in the background. It was tuned to a Christian station, which had promised to air a brief segment about the Let There Be Light project.

Instead, they had sandbagged Sol and turned it into a hit piece.

This was Christian establishment payback. Thus, instead of the interview with Sol and Katy, there was an interview with Doctor Reinhardt Fournier droning on in the background.

"If you ask me," droned the much put-upon Fournier, "this is just another Sol Harkens publicity stunt, and I for one don't feel like being suckered into believing that Sol Harkens, the biggest atheist in the world, has suddenly, pardon the pun, seen the light. And it'll take a lot more than a phone app to change my mind."

Sol grabbed the remote and turned off the TV. "So much for that," he grumbled to himself.

"You burned an awful lot of bridges with the Christian outlets. As for the other outlets, they couldn't care less." Tracee gathered up her briefcase and purse, heading out to her day job. Sol meandered over to the door with her. "You know, when Sylvie and Norm dumped you, I had to rethink all my priorities. I was raised in the church, but somewhere along the way, I don't know. It just wasn't cool. You've reintroduced me to my faith, and I want to thank you for that." She put her arms around Sol and gave him a hug. She whispered, "We'll make this work."

"I know we will. Here, help yourself to a Wipe-Wowie."

"I've already got three," said Tracee.

"You can never have too many," Sol said.

Tracee took the Wipe-Wowie and headed out the door. Then she stopped, turned, and said, "You let me know how this date turns out."

"It's not a date. It's a working dinner," Sol said.

"Uh huh," said Tracee. "And I'm Oprah Winfrey. I want details in the morning."

CHAPTER 17

At just before seven, Sol's Benz pulled into the drive at 1927 Meadowview Court. Sol was wearing a new pair of slacks, a blue silk polo, and a sports jacket that, he hoped, gave him the proper air of casual elegance. He wanted to look good, but that was never a problem for Sol. He wanted to look like he had dressed up for the occasion, but not over-dressed. Just enough to announce his intention that tonight was special.

Sol got out of the car and crossed up to the front door, whose lock had long ago been changed, the key to which he did not possess.

He rang the bell and looked at the two trees in the upper part of the front yard. Both he and Katy had fallen in love with them at first sight. They were literally male and female, and the branches of the larger male tree had intertwined with the branches of the female. They were a couple. And if trees could express love toward one another, theirs was a passionate and permanent one.

The door opened behind him. Sol snapped out of his rev-erie and turned, expecting to see Katy.

And saw the stern visage of his son Gus instead.

"Hello, Father," he greeted him in a no-nonsense tone.

"'Hello, Father'? That's a little formal, isn't it?"

Gus took his father's arm and led him down the flagstone steps that wound their way through the front yard, toward the curb. This was to be a conversation between the two men and, evidently, without punches pulled. "Mom hasn't finished dressing yet," Gus said sternly. "She'll be down in a minute."

"Okay," said Sol.

"You realize this is a school night. I expect her back here by ten."

"I see."

"Sharp."

"Ten o'clock, sharp," said Sol.

"Are we clear on that?" said Gus, doing his best Jack Nicholson from *A Few Good Men.*

"Crystal," said Sol, doing his best Tom Cruise from the same.

"Good."

"Good. Can I come in?"

Gus looked around to make sure no one could hear what he had to say. He pulled Sol a bit farther out onto the flagstone walk, away from the house. "This date is, like, a really big deal to Mom."

"It is to me, too."

"Well," said Gus, "I want you to know. I wasn't in favor of it." He looked his father dead in the eyes. "You've said all the right things. Made all the right moves. But a leopard doesn't change its stripes."

"Spots."

"Whatever. You get my drift. Don't be a jerk, Dad. Ten o'clock. I'll be up, waiting," he said, in the tone of Clint Eastwood saying, "Well, punk, do you feel lucky?"

Just then, the two of them heard the door open up behind them. Katy stepped out into the magic-hour sunlight. She looked, quite simply, ravishing.

The highlights in her hair shone in the last rays of the sun. She wore a simple, blue silk dress that was classically elegant and unbelievably feminine, and it was hard to tell if she was wearing blush or blushing.

"What are you two doing so far down on the lawn?"

"Just, you know, father-son conversation," said Sol.

"Baseball," said Gus.

"Hoops," said his father.

"That sort of thing," said the stern-eyed teenager.

"Great! Well, okay, dinner's on the table." She crossed over to Gus and kissed him on the cheek. "I'll see you and Connor later."

Sol smiled his own gunfighter smile. "See you later."

But Gus was not to be deterred. "Ten o'clock, sharp," he reiterated, before adding the Robert De Niro *I've got my eyes on you* move from *Meet the Parents*.

Sol walked Katy over to the Benz and opened the car door for her. She smiled and thanked him. It had been a long time since he had done that. She slid into the Benz. Sol walked around the front of the car, got in, started it up, and backed down the driveway.

He drove down Meadowview Court, and instead of continuing to Maple Drive, which would have, in turn, led to the main highway leading into town, he turned left on Briarwood and drove down past the meadow that bordered the house and made a left into the parking lot behind the small amphitheater at the end of the meadow.

"Why are we stopping here?"

"Because we're here."

"Here where? You said we were going to a restaurant."

He got out of the car, walked to her side, opened the door, and extended his hand to help her out.

"I said we were going to dinner," he said.

"At a restaurant," Katy said.

"Note to self: I believe I said a very small and exclusive restaurant that just opened."

"I just want to point out, we are in the meadow behind our—behind my house."

"Noted," said Sol.

Katy stumbled in her high heels on the uneven ground of the meadow. Sol took her hand to keep her from falling, but this time, he didn't let go of it. They walked on the flagstone path that led up from the parking lot and into the meadow in front of the small amphitheater. And there, at the height of magic hour, on the bandstand, strung with rope lights twinkling like a thousand stars, was a table set for two. Soft music was playing. The catering company, which had arranged it all, had disappeared, leaving the cloche-covered dinner, lit candles, and a bottle of non-alcoholic champagne on ice.

Sol, holding Katy by the hand, walked her up the stairs. Katy took in the scene, quite simply, blown away.

"Sol," she whispered, "this is amazing."

"You're amazing," he replied. He popped the cork on the non-alcoholic champagne, filled two flutes, and gave one to her.

They clinked glasses.

Katy looked into his eyes. "To us," she said. She quickly corrected herself. "What I mean is, you know, that we're working on this project together. That 'us'. I didn't mean to imply that there was a, a, different 'us.'"

Sol just looked at her and said, "To us."

He pulled out the chair for her, and she sat down, smiling.

He pulled the cloches off the plates, revealing two dinners of grilled salmon topped with pesto, atop a salad of young greens, with fanned avocado slices and supremes of orange segments. It was Katy's favorite dish.

Sol had put together a playlist of songs they had listened to when they were courting.

They talked and laughed and ate their dinners.

A waiter appeared out of nowhere to clear their plates, pour the coffee, and place a plate of profiteroles between them.

"This is the most..." Katy looked away, choking up. "This is so..." Again, she couldn't complete the sentence.

Sol took her hand in his and said, "I think, between two people, it boils down to two lines. One's from Bob Dylan and the other's from Leonard Cohen. Not exactly Matthew and John, but we're talking baby steps, right?"

"I have no idea what you're talking about," Katy said, but she didn't remove her hand from his.

"Maybe they're the most important two things that can be said between a man and a woman, I don't know," said Sol. "One is, 'I owe my heart to you, and that's sayin' it true, and I'll be with you when the deal goes down.' And the other is, simply, 'Hallelujah'. Praise God. Katy, will you do me the unbelievable and totally undeserved honor of becoming my wife, again?"

He reached his hand into his pocket and pulled out a beautiful little box, then opened it, revealing a beautiful diamond engagement ring set with blue sapphires.

Katy began to cry, and then managed to say, "Hallelujah. And yes!"

Sol and Katy stood, embraced, and kissed. They swayed to the music, their silhouettes dark against the last glow of sunset.

They danced, and talked, and laughed, and cried, for hours. Until, finally, Sol looked at his watch and saw that it was ten thirty.

It had seemed that they were only there an hour.

"I'd better get you home," he said. "I've been warned."

He opened the car door for her, then got into the Benz, drove around the corner to Meadowview Court, and pulled into the driveway. Sol opened the door for her again and she stepped into an embrace as they kissed in the driveway.

"Don't go yet," he said. "Why?"

"There are children in that house. They're the enemy. I want you to myself for a little while longer."

He pulled her closer in toward him and they kissed, softly at first and then with growing passion when, suddenly, there was the sound of the front door opening and Gus clearing his throat.

"Hello?" he said. "Ten thirty? School night? Thought we had an understanding?"

"I think we're about to have a new understanding," Sol told him. "Is your brother awake?"

"I think you're changing the subject."

Sol turned to Katy. "What's that thing about 'Spare the rod, spoil the Gus'?"

Katy said nothing, just smiled.

He turned back to Gus. "If your brother's asleep, wake him up. I need to talk to you both."

Katy and Sol sat on the sofa, holding hands. Gus led a very sleepy Connor into the living room. The two of them sat opposite their parents.

"This better be good," said Connor.

"That's what I said," said Gus. But both boys could not help but notice their parents were holding hands.

"This might seem like we're reversing things a bit," said Sol, "but since your Mom and I got divorced, you two have been the men of the family. And what I want to say doesn't just affect your Mom and me, it affects the two of you as well."

"You're gonna cut our allowance?" Connor asked, with twelve-year-old trepidation.

Sol smiled. "I've asked for your mother's hand in marriage. I've asked her to take me back as her husband. We're adults and we don't need anybody's permission, but I would like your blessing. I want us to be a family again."

Connor and Gus just looked at each other.

"This is a little sudden, don't you think?" said Gus.

"You're treading on really thin ice," Sol said.

"Does this mean you're moving back in?" Connor asked excitedly.

"After your Mom and I are married."

"Yahoo!" Connor shouted. He jumped up out of his seat and flew into his mother and father's arms.

Sol looked at Gus, who sat there, staring at his father sternly. "Gus?"

His oldest son broke into a grin. "Psych! Absolutely. I'm just busting your chops."

And he jumped into what had become a group hug.

"The three men I love most," Katy smiled.

"So, it's cool with you guys?" Sol asked.

Connor looked at his parents with a sly grin. "I think it probably calls for a raise in allowance."

Katy laughed. "It probably calls for...It probably calls for...It probably calls for..."

Suddenly, her eyes looked panicked, as she realized she couldn't complete the sentence. Her body began to tremble.

"Katy, what's wrong?!" Sol asked.

Katy's teeth clenched and she began to convulse as if in response to electric shocks jolting through her body. Her eyes rolled back in her head, and she fell into a full grand mal seizure. Sol caught her before she hit the floor, as her body twitched and spasmed. He took his wallet and jammed it between her teeth so she would not bite off her tongue, and shouted out, "Gus, call 9-1-1!"

The fire station was just down the street, and the paramedics arrived within just five minutes. Gently, they lifted Katy onto a gurney and secured her. Sol held her hand as they wheeled her down to the waiting ambulance.

He turned to the boys as they loaded their mother inside. "Gus, take care of your brother. We'll call you from the hospital."

"Is Mom gonna be okay?" Connor asked in a panic.

"Absolutely," Sol said, with as much conviction as he could muster.

But Gus had burned into his mind the single most frightening moment of his childhood. "That's what happened to Davey!" he cried. "He had a seizure, just like that!"

"Gus!" said Sol, as loudly and forcefully as he could, to snap his son out of the panic that had swept over him. "You and your brother say a prayer for your mom. I'll call you from the hospital."

Suddenly, Gus was no longer the precocious teenager, but a frightened child once again. He and Connor rushed into their father's arms.

"God's not gonna let this happen again, is he, Dad?" Gus asked.

Sol was fighting down his own panic. "I don't know, son. That's where those prayers of yours come in. Go back inside now. Mom's gonna be okay."

Gus took his little brother's hand, and they walked back into the house as the paramedics closed the door of the ambulance with Sol and Katy inside. Katy looked up to Sol. He took her hand and kissed it.

"I'm with you now, Katy. Now it's my turn to take care of you."

CHAPTER 18

Except for the fact that she's just gone through a full grand mal seizure, Katy looks great, Sol thought. *It's the hospital that looks like crap.*

There's a stage that you get to after the person you love more than life itself has their eyes roll back in their head and every electric current in their body goes haywire, their teeth clench, their muscles spasm, and you believe they're going to explode. Amazingly, that only lasts less than a minute, the first time around. And then they're fine. Their color returns, they joke with you sometimes they can't understand why you look so worried because they really weren't there while the seizure took place. They didn't see what you saw. Their hearts didn't go into their throats. They didn't pray, "Oh, no, dear God, please, no, not again."

They simply weren't there.

Their muscles are a little sore from the spasms.

If they bumped their head, that hurts.

But outside of that, they feel fine.

They just can't understand why you look so shaken when they feel so good.

There's the ride to the hospital in the ambulance, and by the time they arrive, they can't understand why they're strapped to a gurney.

And since the seizure is over and the life-threatening emergency has ended, the pace slows, suddenly, to something less than glacial. There are forms to be filled out, insurance cards to be copied, release forms to be signed. Then you're curtained off in a cubicle in the emergency room. And, if you live by a big city, you listen to the screams of the gunshot-wound victims, the women who have just gone into unexpected labor, the kid who was knifed by a classmate…

And you wait.

Because you're not bleeding to death; they are.

And after a while, the person who's gone through the seizure is suddenly hit, as if they've just been run over by a Mack Truck, and a fatigue sets in unlike any they have ever known and blessedly, they drift off to sleep.

Being a novice at prayer, Sol had run out of prayers. There are only so many times you can say, "Please, God, spare her. Dear God, please, just when we've gotten back together and figured things out, please, dear God, if you have to take someone, anyone, for some kind of purpose, please take my life, not hers."

There is prayer as supplication.

There is prayer as unadulterated bargaining.

And finally, there is the prayer of acceptance. "Thy will be done. Hallelujah."

And after that, if you're not used to reading the Bible or a newbie in terms of the Psalms, you quite simply run out of prayers and you begin to notice décor.

You begin to wonder why all hospitals are painted the same sickly lime color. You wonder who thought that was a good idea.

You begin to ponder the odd hospital gown patterns.

You notice the smells of antiseptic and floor polish.

You try to get someone's attention. You try to explain, "My wife just had a seizure."

If you really want to push it, you tell them your child died from a brain tumor, which started with exactly the same kind of seizure. But if you push it too hard with someone who's nearing end of shift, who's put up with shooting victims, abused wives and children, the mangled body of a car accident, the drug overdose of some knucklehead kid who thought they were just partying, you find yourself running your head against a brick wall.

And then, finally, after you've been there for about three hours, the tests begin.

You wait while they roll your loved one down to the MRI.

MRI technicians rarely have a sense of urgency about them. Whether it's a torn rotator cuff or a possible brain tumor, it's basically the same gig, and most of the time, thankfully, it's not a brain tumor. Or, if it is, it's benign. Or, if it's malignant, it's a garden-variety malignancy. Rare tumors are called rare because they are, well, rare. So, the sense of urgency of a medic on the battlefield saving his or her comrade in arms is noticeably absent.

There is some banter, some small talk. The patient is transferred from gurney to razor-thin bed. To protect them from the noise and the claustrophobia, they get a kind of blindfold and a set of headphones, from which they can choose heavy metal, classic rock, light symphonic, or comedy retreads. If they're sensing a feeling of claustrophobia, they can even get a bit of Valium.

The sound is, indeed, irritating. The process, though bearable, is not at all pleasant.

But mainly, it's the waiting.

Because the tests, having been taken—blood samples, vitals, MRIs, X-rays—whatever your insurance will allow, have to be analyzed by a doctor, whose expertise qualifies them to deliver the news, good or bad.

"Nothing to worry about," or "Get your affairs in order."

By the time that happens and the doctor gets to the room to which you have been transferred, you have been there six or seven hours.

Such was the case with Katy Harkens.

Sol called in every big gun he knew, but it's amazing how big guns can find themselves limited by small bureaucracies.

The head neurologist at Mount Sinai might not pull much weight at New Haven. He might know somebody who does, but they may be on vacation, or because they're not on call, they may simply not be answering calls.

And so, you wait.

And you're back to critiquing the décor.

At eight o'clock the next morning, a kindly looking doctor in his mid-fifties with an incongruously southern accent for New Haven made his entrance into Katy's room. He had a goatee and mustache, a somewhat-receding hairline, and a pleasing, good-ol'-boy look about him. He looked like he'd be more at home at a barbecue, saying, "I'll take mine medium-rare" and pulling a longneck out of an ice chest, than introducing himself as a physician.

But, indeed, he was not at a barbecue.

"I'm Doctor Corey. How are you doing..." He checked her medical chart before finishing. "Uh, Katy?"

"I actually feel pretty good. But why don't you tell me?" She smiled and it was as if she'd never been convulsing on her living room floor. Sol knew it was just a trick of time.

Doctor Corey smiled a kindly smile and, in his Texan accent, said, "We've had a chance to study the MRI and the CT scan, and we've gotten a pretty detailed look at your blood work."

Sol wanted to cut to the chase. He didn't like prologues. And so, he interrupted. "Excuse me, Doctor, but what is your specialty? No offense."

Doctor Corey looked at him evenly and uttered the three words you definitely don't want to hear after the person you love has had a full grand mal seizure. "I'm an oncologist."

Sol felt the déjà vu punch in his gut. "Oh, no. Oh, no," he said again.

But his reaction was that of a man in love.

Katy's reaction was that of a mother. Katy reacted as the mother of a child who had died of cancer.

She gasped. Her hand involuntarily rose to her mouth, as if to prevent the words from coming out. She shook her head back and forth, in horror of the truth she was about to utter. "It was me, wasn't it? I gave it to him, didn't I, Doctor? I gave our son cancer."

Sol heard the words, and the penny dropped for him as well. And, Lord help him, he didn't care. At this moment, he only cared about the woman he loved.

Doctor Corey, who was truly a compassionate man and whose job it was to deliver the news no one ever wanted to get, stepped forward, leaned in toward Katy, and reassured her. "That is absolutely not true, Mrs. Harkens."

Katy was shaking her head back and forth. He knew he needed to get her attention.

"Mrs. Harkens," Doctor Corey said. "I need you to look at me. Mrs. Harkens. Look at me."

Katy looked at him.

"I need you to listen and understand what I'm saying to you. Will you do that, Mrs. Harkens?"

Katy nodded her head.

Then Doctor Corey turned to Sol. "Mr. Harkens?" he said, not recognizing Sol as the famous PhD of atheism.

Sol nodded his head as well. He and Katy were being obedient children. Someone older and wiser was about to impart a truth upon them.

Confident in having gotten their attention, Doctor Corey proceeded. "The blood work indicates that you have Li-Fraumeni syndrome. The syndrome is most often caused by inherited mutations in the gene for p53."

Katy shook her head as if he were speaking Japanese. "Which means what, in English?"

It was then that Sol noticed that Doctor Corey was clutching the medical chart to his chest like a plate of armor to protect his own emotional well-being. He did not take this as a good sign.

"P53," said Doctor Corey, "is the gene that stops the growth of abnormal cells. You have that mutation. You didn't give your son cancer, ma'am, do you understand?"

Katy shook her head no, afraid even to speak.

"You have an inherited gene," explained the doctor, "that you got from one of your ancestors. Sometimes it skips a generation, sometimes two or three."

"So, this syndrome is what caused the seizure?" Sol asked. He was clutching at straws now. Syndromes, any syndromes, sounded better than what he feared the most.

"No," said Doctor Corey, dashing both of their hopes.

Both Katy and Sol noticed that the good doctor took a deep breath, and they knew he did so because he was about to drop the hammer. Now he was about to do the thing he hated most about his job.

"People with Li-Fraumeni syndrome are susceptible to various types of cancer, including brain tumors."

There. He had said it in one breath.

Unfortunately, it was not the worst of what he had to deliver, and so, he took another breath. "Which, I'm afraid, is what you have. It's called a glioblastoma multiforme."

He paused as if that one breath had run out. As if whatever he had just said in Latin required yet another act to steel his own nerves, to deliver the worst news of all. The breath he took was audible, and with it, they saw his chest expand. "It's a stage four cancer."

"Oh my God," said Sol. "Oh my God."

Instinctively, he reached for Katy, as if they were both about to go over a cliff and he wanted them to do it together. Katy, however, was ramrod-stiff.

She looked Corey straight in the eyes, determined to gather information, not focus on emotion. "What are my chances, Doctor? And please, don't sugarcoat anything. I'm a big girl. I have decisions to make. I need to know."

Doctor Corey nodded his head several times. He looked down, and it seemed to Sol that he clutched Katy's chart even more tightly to his chest. "Unfortunately," he said, in the gentlest voice he could muster, "the prospects are not good." He looked at them both, from one to another. "This is a very virulent tumor. It's quite advanced." And now it seemed like he was a drowning man who had finally reached a lifeboat. He could cling to doctor-speak, and it would save him from drowning in the human tragedy with which he dealt from day to day. He could deliver a lecture, of sorts. Simple facts.

"The tumor," he knitted his fingers together to demonstrate, "is interwoven with normal brain cells to such an extent that I wouldn't recommend surgery." He paused to gauge whether they understood what he had just said. He had just told them that the tumor was inoperable. The worst was over. He had just delivered a death sentence, and anything he said after that was anticlimactic. "There is an experimental protocol that involves chemotherapy, but quite honestly, I don't believe we'd be talking about a cure. We'd be talking about buying you extra time."

Sol, unlike Doctor Corey, had not yet reached the lifeboat, or even a life preserver. He was still thrashing about in a sea of tragedy, hoping to find anything to which to cling. "How much extra time?" he said.

"Months," said Doctor Corey. "Possibly a year."

Remarkably, Katy felt devoid of emotion. And without it, she asked, "How much time do I have?"

Silently, Doctor Corey thanked all the gods that be for these two rational beings. There was no crying, no gasps, no anguished cries of pain, simply straightforward questions. How much time did she have? "Months. There's a milder form of chemo that we could do, however, I'm not sure what the benefit would be."

Sol was still swimming for a life preserver, unsure as to whether it existed or whether it was the mirage that drowning men see. "What about this experimental program? Somebody has to have survived this thing!"

Doctor Corey took another breath. "Five percent, maybe less."

Sol reacted as if he had just won the lottery. "Then she's gonna be part of the five percent, that's all!" he said with certainty. He looked at Katy, then Doctor Corey, and pointed at the woman he loved. "This is the strongest woman I've ever met in my life, Doctor. She *makes* miracles happen!"

Doctor Corey's smile carried no joy in it, simply the compassion of a wise man for a fool. There was a silence that hung in the air. Doctor Corey refused to confirm that the life preserver Sol had just chosen to cling to was anything more than a mirage.

Katy, however, was a mother, and mothers are practical. They want to know if they have to pack a lunch. Are snacks allowed? Will my child need a sweater or a jacket, and what time will they be home?

"Outside of just having had a seizure and being in a hospital," she said, "which I hate, I really feel fine! So my question is, how long do I have before I don't feel fine?"

Katy fixed Doctor Corey's eyes with her own, as if by force of will refusing to allow him to look away. He held her gaze just as he held her chart up to his chest.

"I wish I could give you exact answers, Mrs. Harkens, but I just can't. It's why they call medicine an art. It's not like mathematics. I can't tell you with certitude that two and two make four. Sometimes, they make six. Sometimes, two and two add up to only three."

Katy nodded her head, understanding, finally letting him off the hook.

In compensation, perhaps, for her consideration, Doctor Corey offered up the only thing he had. "We certainly have drugs that can keep you comfortable once the pain sets in, if that's what you're thinking about."

"No," Katy said. That's not what I'm thinking about at all."

Man, does this guy not know Katy at all, Sol thought.

Katy continued. "I'm thinking about planning a wedding, not a funeral." Katy turned her gaze to Sol and fixed him with it. He had to understand what she was saying too. "Sol, whatever time I have left, I need to spend it doing three things: preparing for eternity, ensuring the success of Let There Be Light, and loving my boys and you."

CHAPTER 19

The meadow behind their home, the home in which Sol and Katy's three boys had been born, the home in which one had been buried, lay atop a slight rise that fed down into another meadow below, which was the heart of their small community. It was the place where Fourth of July picnics, barbecues, and fireworks were held. The place of farmer's markets in the autumn and Christmas celebrations in the snow. Where, bedecked with colored lights, an old Mr. Havermeyer in a well-worn Santa suit and white beard still managed to fool the smallest children on the block that Santa was really there in the meadow behind their homes, handing out candy canes. And in the spring, there were Easter egg rolls and hunts ringing in the first joys of spring.

Now, the first of the autumn leaves were turning gold and orange. Summer was gone and with it, the joys of children that played without a care in the world as they returned to the routine of school and carpools, the normalcy that separated vacations from reality.

The bandstand at the bottom of the meadow, or as some referred to it in a more grandiose manner, the amphitheater, was now festooned with white twinkle lights and the flowers of autumn harvest. There was a small crowd of women in sundresses, for the bite of the Connecticut autumn was late this year and the sun still bestowed its blessings. There were perhaps thirty family members and the closest of friends. There was nothing raucous, nor was there really a sense of solemnity. More than all else, there was a sense of awe. In the midst of the certitude of death, Katy and Sol were determined to celebrate life.

The ravages of her disease had not yet set in, and Katy looked radiant in a soft, pastel dress. Sol, Gus, and Connor had matching suits, pale blue shirts, and no ties. There was a simple, East Coast elegance about them all. They were festive, not formal, in appearance.

Pastor Vinny was there, and one could only say, judging by his appearance, that while one could take the pastor out of the Mob, it appeared impossible to take the Mafioso wiseguy out of the pastor. The suit was sharkskin, one hundred percent wiseguy elegance.

Tracee was there as the only bridesmaid.

Laurie, Pastor Vinny's wife, was the matron of honor.

The hour of the wedding, chosen carefully by Tracee's practiced publicist's eye, was magic hour, the exact time of day to make everyone look as though they were bathed in gold.

And there was a surprise.

Tracee's aunt, LaVonne, had gone to school with a young girl who would become one of the most famous singers in the world, Dionne Warwick. Tracee had prevailed upon her to tell the story of Katy and Sol.

And so, there she was, incongruously, on the tiny bandstand in the meadow behind Katy and Sol's home. Her short white hair and gleaming smile made her look positively angelic. She was Mother Earth incarnate, the wise grandma of your dreams. Dionne Warwick took Katy and Sol both by the hand, as if they were her children, and said, "When I heard from my childhood friend LaVonne that the most famous atheist in the world had found Jesus and was remarrying his Christian wife, I said, 'This is one wedding I have got to sing at.'"

She nodded to her road manager in the wings, who pressed the playback button. Violin strings filled the air along with a beat that could only be called a Dionne Warwick beat. She closed her eyes and began to hum, and there was that voice, that unmistakable voice that had said, "Whenever I wake up, before I put on my makeup, I say a little prayer for you..." The same voice that had asked if you knew the way to San Jose, that declared that what the world needs now is love, sweet love, that had asked Alfie what it was all about, and that, with a broken heart, had said, "I'll never fall in love again."

Sol and Katy began to sway in the embrace of her voice as Dionne sang a song she had written just for their special day.

"I'm gonna share a little secret,
Something common, something real.
True love is not impossible,
It is something you must feel.
"When the promise
Of an answer
Is not always clear,
Look up and say,
'Let there be light,'
Let your love shine bright.
'Let there be light,'
Let your light shine bright.
If you trust in faith,
Your worries will fade away
Into the light..."

Dionne held their hands as she sang it, like a lullaby to her children. She looked into their eyes with each lyric, and what was so moving was not just the beauty of her voice, made even more mellow with the years, but the truth to which they were all now bearing witness, that, in the face of darkness, they would say, as one, "Let there be light."

She finished the song and kissed Katy on her cheek, then Sol. Ever the showwoman, she signaled over to the wiseguy preacher. "Pastor Vinny, take it away."

The calm silence following the song may have disturbed another performer, however, it was clear that the silence was one of awe. Most of the guests were too busy wiping away a tear or two to applaud. Pastor Vinny, one of the toughest guys to come out of Bensonhurst, had to clear his throat before beginning, so moved was he by the song written for his parishioners.

"Family and friends," Pastor Vinny began, "we are here to celebrate the love of Katy and Sol." He looked over at Connor and Gus. "Known to y'uz guys as 'Mom and Dad.' Best Man, do ya have the ring?"

Gus stepped forward and handed the ring to Sol.

Pastor Vinny looked at Sol and said so only he could hear, "I used to know a guy who fenced these. He could've gotten it for ya cheaper." Then he spoke so all could hear.

"Dis ring, like your love, is like da love of God. It has no beginning," he looked at Katy, holding her eyes with his. "And it certainly has no end. Sol, place dis ring on Katy's finger, an' repeat after me. I, Sol, take this woman, Katy—"

Sol took Katy's hand in his, looked into her eyes, and saw both the girl whom he'd fallen in love with twenty years before and the woman whom he so desperately loved at this moment. He wanted to make every word count, to engrave it in both their hearts. "I, Sol, take *this* woman, Katy."

"To be my lawfully wedded wife," said Pastor Vinny.

"To be my lawfully wedded wife," repeated Sol happily.

"To have an' to hold, forsaking all others."

"To have and to hold, forsaking all others."

"For richer or for poorer," said Pastor Vinny, "for better or for worse."

"For richer or for poorer. For better or for worse."

Pastor Vinny used every bit of strength he had to keep his voice from cracking as he said, "In sickness and in health, 'til death do us part."

Here and there, in the audience of loved ones, people fought back sobs, but Sol and Katy were having none of it.

"You can knock out that last bit," Sol said, smiling. "Been there, done that. And what you call death doesn't get a vote in this." Then he turned to Katy, smiling like a schoolboy with his first love. "The answer is, 'I do.'"

Katy smiled, even broader. "I'll second that. 'I do,' too."

Pastor Vinny nodded, then grinned from ear to ear, thanking the Lord that the tough part was over. "Den we can cut to da good stuff. By da power vested in me by da court on high, as well as da court of man, I pronounce you bot' man and wife! You may now kiss da bride."

Sol took Katy in his arms, drew her to him, and they kissed what may have been the sweetest, purest kiss any bride and groom may ever have known.

Photos were snapped, hankies dabbed away tears, someone cried out, "*Mazel tov!*" and someone else yelled out, "Wrong wedding!"

Everyone was laughing, for while others may have only spotted the dark cloud, they were reveling in the silver lining.

Then a cell phone went off.

"Play that funky music, white boy...

Wild Cherry's 'Play That Funky Music,' ringtone signaled that it was Tracee's incoming call. She fumbled in her purse for the phone, apologizing profusely as the plaintive lyrics sprang forth from her clutch.

"I am *so* sorry!" Tracee said, as the chorus repeated and Wild Cherry once again exhorted that white boy to play that funky music. "I will turn this off!"

Finally, she fished the Black Cherry-spewing phone out of her purse. She glanced at the caller ID. "I *can't* turn this off!" She walked a few steps up the meadow from the celebrating congregants and spoke into her phone, first turning to Sol and Katy, saying, "You two look *fabulous*, by the way!"

Having complimented the bride and groom, she turned her attention to her caller. "Hi...Yes, this is Tracee...You're kidding!...You're not kidding?!...When?!...Absolutely! Absolutely!...Thank you so much! They'll be there! Well, they just got married, but they'll still be there! Thank you, again!" She hung up and turned around. Sol, Katy, Connor, Gus, Pastor Vinny, Dionne Warwick, and all the guests were looking at her with a mixture of shock, horror, and expectation.

Tracee was only looking over at Sol and Katy, unable to contain her excitement. "Your honeymoon plans just got changed! You're doing Sean Hannity, tomorrow. Both of you! Fourteen million listeners on his radio program, three million viewers on his TV show! This is the best way I can think of for you guys to launch your app!"

Sol and Katy spent their wedding night at the Plaza and then cabbed it, at ten o'clock in the morning, to 48th and Avenue of the Americas. There were passes waiting for them at the security desk, and a production assistant came down to meet them. After being escorted to the elevator, they were sitting opposite Sean Hannity. His office was filled with the friendly clutter of an everyday guy, a former construction worker who was now one of the most recognizable broadcasters in the world. He wore a pair of blue jeans, a sports shirt, and a blazer, and sipped from a cup of coffee with his company's logo on it.

He looked at Sol and Katy, and said, "Are you guys ready for the amount of heat you're gonna take for this?"

Katy, who was holding hands with Sol, smiled at Sean and said, "I think we can handle it."

"I hope so," Hannity said, in an accent that bespoke his Hampstead, Long Island, roots. He continued as if he couldn't believe what he was about to say. "You guys actually intend to proselytize to—"

"To the exact same kids ISIS is targeting," Sol said. "Absolutely. I mean, we want to reach everybody, but especially them."

"Yeah," said Hannity. "But you're actually going to be out there, trying to convert kids to Christianity?"

"Sure," said Katy. "Why not?"

"You're going to have all kinds of people saying you have to respect diversity and what right do you have to impose your religious beliefs on somebody else."

"What right does ISIS have to cut people's heads off?" Sol asked.

"All we want to do is spread light into darkness," Katy added.

Hannity looked from one Harkens to the other. These were two intelligent, sophisticated people. How could they possibly be this naïve?

As if reading his thoughts, Sol said, "Nobody has to convert to anything. I mean, unlike ISIS, it's not a convert-or-die proposition."

"And," said Katy, "if they just text 'LTBL,' they'll be feeding their neighbors."

"But if they want to talk to somebody about the love of Christ," said the world's most famous former atheist, "we'll have people standing by, without apologies."

Hannity just shook his head. He knew how sick Katy was. He knew exactly how much courage it took to be doing what they were about to do. He took another sip of his coffee, leaned back in his chair, and thought for a beat. "Let me ask you a question. Is anybody going to be covering this, Christmas Eve, when that band of light goes around the globe?"

Sol thought of every news outlet they had gone to, of every polite no, every condescending sneer, every dismissive "You guys must be out of your minds." He smiled, not without a little bitterness, and said, "So far, no one's covering it, not even a little bit."

With that, Hannity leaned forward in his chair. "Well, that just changed. I'd be honored to spend Christmas Eve with you guys. We'll do a three-hour special. I'll get on the horn to our head of programming, and I guarantee, he'll get onboard with it. And we reach almost every country on Earth. What do you say?"

CHAPTER 20

There was nothing pretty about the months leading up to Christmas.

Katy began her chemotherapy treatments. In the shower, clumps of her hair cascaded down and clogged the drain. Sol would hold her forehead as she vomited into the toilet. He would rock her, back and forth, between waves of nausea. Her athletic body grew thinner, until her ribs stuck out and her shoulder blades protruded.

She wore scarves now, to cover the fact that she was bald.

When she felt up to it, she helped the boys with their homework.

They prayed each night at dinner, even though she could barely choke down a bite. And they prayed again with their pajama-clad children as they kissed their boys good night.

And so it went. All of their time was spent working with Sally Darwan on the app, lining up chat rooms and churches around the country, and coordinating the Christmas Eve broadcast with Hannity and his staff.

Both Katy and Sol were aware of how little time they had left, and not just until the broadcast. They wanted to spend as much time as possible with their boys. They wanted to savor each sweet memory, each smile, each laugh, each prayer. Still, it seemed there were never enough hours in each given day.

One night after dinner, Sol said, "I have to go to the pharmacy and pick up some meds for Mom before they close." He hugged and kissed each of his sons, who hugged and kissed him back. "Good night, you guys."

Sol left the house, got into his Benz, and drove until he was out of sight of their home. Then he pulled over and sobbed like a child. He pounded his fists against the steering wheel. He shouted a cry of anguish out into the night. It wasn't a curse, it wasn't a plea for mercy. There was no condemnation to it. And no hope.

It was, in the words of the Leonard Cohen song, nothing more than a cold and broken hallelujah.

After loosing the fear and anger inside himself onto the steering wheel, he dried his eyes, started the engine back up, and drove to the pharmacy.

Back in their home, Katy, exhausted, could hold her head up no longer. "I'm going to sleep. Good night, my sweet boys." She had been reading on the couch, keeping watch over the two boys as they played chess on the coffee table in front of her. Katy pulled off her glasses, closed her book, and laid them both on the side table as she gingerly stood up.

It was hard for her to walk, but she bent over to each boy and kissed them. They hugged her, feeling how frail she had become.

She had started her halting journey out of the living room when Gus spoke.

"Mom?"

Katy turned in the doorway and leaned against it. "Yes, sweetheart?"

"Are you...are you gonna get better?"

Katy put a cocky grin on her face and crossed her arms. "I think I'm pretty good right now."

"You know what I mean," Gus said, somber.

"We've been praying really hard, Mom," said Connor.

Katy crossed back toward her boys and gingerly knelt down in front of where they were sitting on the couch.

"I know," she said. "And don't think I haven't felt those prayers, because I have. They're what give me strength."

"Then God'll answer our prayers, right?" said Gus.

"God always answers our prayers," Katy said. "Sometimes, we just don't understand the answer."

Gus screwed up his mouth and said, "That doesn't make any sense."

Katy looked at him evenly, then asked, "You know how many times Jesus prayed in the Garden of Gethsemane?"

"Three times."

"That's right." She looked at Connor. "And what did he pray for?"

"That God would lift his burden," her youngest son answered.

"That he wouldn't have to die on the cross," Gus said, hoping that Jesus was listening to their conversation as well.

Katy took both her sons' hands in hers. "He prayed for God's will to be done. And it was God's will, God's plan, that Jesus's life and what we call death would bring salvation to all mankind." She looked from one to the other. "So, did God answer Jesus's prayers?"

The boys were fighting back tears.

"I guess so," said Connor.

Katy stroked her youngest's face. "Where's your brother Davey, Connor?"

"In Heaven."

"And how do you know?"

"Because Daddy saw him there," said Connor. It was a simple statement, not of belief or faith, but fact. Daddy had seen his brother there.

"Absolutely. So there's nothing to be afraid of, is there?"

"I don't care about Heaven!" Connor blurted out, no longer a preteen, but a little boy clinging to his mother. "I just don't want you to die, Mommy!"

Katy kissed his forehead. "I don't think there's any such thing as death." She looked from one boy to the other. In her calmest voice, she explained, "When I'm in the next room and you can't see me, does that mean I'm dead? Or am I just in the next room?"

"You're just in the next room," Connor answered.

"That's right," Katy said. She stood up and kissed Connor and Gus and then walked as steadily as she could toward the door that led to the hallway to her room. She turned back to her boys. "I'm just in the next room. Still loving you, still watching over you. Time to get some sleep, okay?"

"Okay," said Connor.

She looked at Gus. "Okay?"

"Yeah," he answered.

"Okay. I'll be just in the next room. Goodnight, my sweet boys."

Katy was too weak to travel into Manhattan on Christmas Eve. And so, it was decided that Sean Hannity would broadcast from his studio and a remote crew would be dispatched to Sol and Katy's home in Connecticut, where they, their boys, their neighbors, Tracee, Pastor Vinny, his wife Laurie, and Sally Darwan would do a remote for the broadcast.

The crew arrived in the late afternoon and set up in the backyard. They rearranged the outdoor furniture and situated the camera to one side of the yard, where the evergreen trees provided a cozy, snow-dusted backdrop.

Neighbors from up and down the block turned out to help and also participate in the big event. They brought cookies and hot chocolate to share. There was a festive feel, and excitement filled the cold night air.

Unfortunately, Katy was so weak, she could barely hold her head up. Situated on the couch with Sol, Katy lay her head on his shoulder as she watched the interview with Sally Darwan. The tumor was pressed up against Broca's area—that portion of the brain responsible for speech—making it impossible for her to give any kind of interview and share her hard work. Sol, for his part, said there was no way he would appear on camera, either. Sally would explain the app and share more of their project with the world so people watching could download it, and Sean would do the heavy lifting. But Katy and Sol would be there to celebrate and bear witness to what Katy had accomplished and to what their love had created.

In the studio on Sixth and 48th, the floor manager counted down and pointed his finger at Sean Hannity when the familiar logo came up. Hannity looked into the camera. "Welcome to a three-hour special edition of *Hannity* where, tonight, history is being made all over the world. I'm sure by now, everyone has heard the incredible story of Sol and Katy Harkens and their Let There Be Light project."

Sol, Katy, the boys, the neighbors—everyone watched the broadcast on a monitor set up in the backyard and watched the images from outer space from the deal they had made with NASA. The impossible dream they had dreamed in Sol's loft apartment was coming to fruition as the pinpricks of lights going on around the world began to appear.

Sean continued his commentary. "Well, at three a.m. this morning on Christmas Island, a band of light visible from outer space began to move around the world. From New Zealand to Russia, to Australia, Japan, and amazingly, in North Korea? How did anyone hear about this in North Korea?! With us tonight, from their home in Connecticut, are Sol and Katy Harkens and Sally Darwan, head of NewComHiTech, which designed the app that is making this extraordinary night possible."

The stage manager in Katy and Sol's backyard pointed at Sally, who sat in a director's chair. On cue, she explained how the app worked, how, no matter where you were on Earth, it told you when your location was the darkest spot on Earth. "And that," she said, "is when you turn your flashlight up to the heavens, and we spread light into the darkness and take a selfie for God. A band of light, encircling the globe on Christmas Eve. And by texting the letters 'LTBL,' you will be automatically giving one of the most beautiful Christmas gifts imaginable: You will be donating food to your local food bank. You will be feeding the hungry. And you will be feeding the spiritually hungry for the knowledge and love of God, because simply by clicking the app, you will be put in touch with a volunteer counselor who will pray with you, answer your questions, refer you to scripture, or send you literature. I can't think of a more meaningful way to spend Christmas Eve."

As Sally continued to explain the app, and Sean continued his interview with her, Katy suddenly got a worried look on her face.

"Sol?"

LET THERE BE LIGHT   229

"What's wrong, baby, are you okay?" Sol asked, cradling her in his arms.

"What if no one used the app?" Her breathing was slow and labored.

"What do you mean?"

"What if it's all a giant dud?" she asked, her speech slurred. "What if we gave a party and nobody came?"

"Look," Sol said, and pointed to the monitor, where footage was being screened of a band of light encircling the globe.

"And this," Sean Hannity said on the monitor, "is the band of light as it looked, in time-lapse photography, spreading all over the world! Pockets of light everywhere, not a thousand points of light, but millions of points of light, illuminating the darkness! Even throughout the Middle East! In ISIS-occupied Syria and Iraq! And now, in New York City, it's our turn. On the East Coast of the United States!"

Sally took her iPhone out and looked at the app, as did Connor and Gus and all their friends and neighbors in the backyard.

"It's almost time!" she shouted out. "Five...Four...Three... Two...And...Now!"

Everyone in the backyard turned on their phones' lights and aimed them skyward. On the monitor sharing the satellite's point of view, the entire Eastern Seaboard of the United States lit up.

Hannity shouted, "Hello, New York! New Jersey! Connecticut! And all the way down to Florida!"

As the light on the screen spread across the United States, Sol held Katy against his chest. He was looking at the monitor and the ever-spreading band of light. "You did it, my darling Kate! You made it happen!"

Katy's eyes were closed, but she was smiling.

Gus and Connor watched in awe as more and more lights appeared on the satellite view on the monitor. And as the light spread across the country, Connor, in his angelic, twelve-year-old voice, began to sing.

"Silent night
Holy night..."

Without prompting, the cameraman, the sound man, the floor manager, Pastor Vinny, Laurie, Gus, Tracee, and all their neighbors joined in.

Sol kissed Katy's forehead as their homegrown heavenly chorus sang.

"'Round yon virgin,
mother and child.
Holy infant,
so tender and mild..."

With her eyes closed, Katy smiled the most beatific smile Sol had ever seen. "It's so beautiful," she whispered. "It's so beautiful!"

She wasn't talking about the singing. Her head slowly slumped against Sol's chest.

"Katy?" he whispered. "Katy?"

He rocked her back and forth as their backyard choir sang.

"Sleep in heavenly peace,
Sleep in heavenly peace..."

And Katy's soul, no longer needing her tired and worn out body, saw the light.

The End

Dan Gordon, on set for the filming of
Let There Be Light. Photo by Zach Brutsch

Dan Gordon is the screenwriter of such movies as *The Hurricane* (Denzel Washington), *Wyatt Earp* (Kevin Costner), *Murder in the First* (Kevin Bacon and Gary Oldman), and *Passenger 57* (Wesley Snipes), and was the head writer on the Michael Landon television series, *Highway to Heaven*. *Let There Be Light* is Gordon's seventeenth feature length film, and ninth novel. He has five produced plays, which have appeared Off and On Broadway and in the West End of London, including Irena's Vow, nominated for Best Broadway Play by the Outer Critics Circle Awards. He is also cofounder of the Zaki Gordon Cinematic Arts Center at Liberty University.

CPSIA information can be obtained
at www.ICGtesting.com
Printed in the USA
LVOW11s0306241117
557348LV00001B/10/P